STEWARDSHIP IN CONTEMPORARY LIFE

STEWARDSHIP IN

CONTEMPORARY LIFE

Edited by

T. K. THOMPSON

ASSOCIATION PRESS · NEW YORK

STEWARDSHIP IN CONTEMPORARY LIFE

Copyright © 1965 by
National Board of Young Men's Christian Associations

Association Press   291 Broadway   New York   N.Y.   10007

Price, cloth edition, $4.95
Publisher's cloth edition stock number: 1572

Price, paper edition, $1.95

Publisher's paperback stock number: W445
Library of Congress catalog card number: 65-11094

Printed in the United States of America

Contents

PART II

Corporate Stewardship

JOSEPH C. McLELLAND

Introduction

STEWARDSHIP, in its Christian sense, is almost impossible to define. Etymologically the meaning is simple enough; it comes from the Anglo-Saxon *stye-ward,* meaning an enclosure for livestock. This root meaning of a person who takes care of the property of another is used to translate the Greek word *oikonomomos,* which literally means "manager of a house." Stewardship usually involves three concepts: a responsible servant, a definite entrustment, and a final accounting. In Christian terms, this means that God entrusts to man all that he has; the Christian is responsible to God for how he handles all these entrustments.

The difficulty in defining the term stewardship comes in setting limits to the meaning. Paul used the term not only for the individual, but for the city official and even for God's plan of the ages. Though the Greek word points to the ordering of the household, it also has been broadened from the economic sense to include almost all the affairs of life. In this book, stewardship will be used in a variety of ways. However, the understanding of the Greek root, order in the management of a household, is basic.

Stewardship, in this sense, is an inescapable responsibility of every man. There must be some principle by which he orders his life, even if that principle is so vague as to mean little more than eating or sleeping whenever he gets the chance.

Stewardship applies to groups as well as to individuals. The chapters prepared by Dr. Joseph McLelland show that in modern life many of the basic decisions are hammered out in the group process through congregations, labor unions, political parties, legislative assemblies, and the United Nations. Responsible participation in the decision-making process through groups is part of the stewardship of every individual Christian.

Dr. Theophilus M. Taylor of the General Council of the United Presbyterian Church, U.S.A., formerly a professor of New Testament at Pittsburgh Theological Seminary, Pittsburgh, Pennsylvania, has given the basic biblical background for stewardship. He has set his discussion in the context of Paul's description of God who has revealed his plan of the ages in Jesus Christ. The description of God as "Steward" has many limitations. There is no ultimate "owner" above God; nor will God be called upon to render a final accounting. However, God has a "plan of the ages" not unlike the wise householder who has a plan of housekeeping. A part of God's plan is the calling of servant-stewards who act responsibly as junior partners with him in his plan of creation and redemption. God calls men together into churches in order that they may fulfill functions of worship, service, and fellowship.

However, it is easy for man to fall into idolatries even in connection with his service in the Church of Jesus Christ. Dr. James Gustafson, professor of Christian ethics at Yale Divinity School, points to many of these idolatries, forms of institutional self-worship expressed in techniques of evangelism and stewardship. People frequently join the church for the wrong reasons and stay out of the church for the wrong reasons. Stewardship leaders frequently fall into the idolatry of assuming that giving to the church is giving to God.

Nevertheless, some kind of church structure is necessary to carry out the will of God revealed in Christ. Dr. Spencer P. Austin shows that although the present denominational structure in America is not necessarily the will of God, some kind of formal, responsible, corporate body is necessary to fulfill Christ's commands for mission and service in the world. If the church can be judged renewed from within by the power of the Holy Spirit, the denomination may indeed be Christ's instrument for his work in the world.

The chapters which make up this book were, with the exception of "Good Stewards of God's Grace," lectures given at a Workshop on Benevolence Promotion, held under the sponsorship of the Department of Stewardship and Benevolence of the National Council of Churches at Westminster College, University of Western Ontario, London, Ontario, in July, 1964. The conference was under the chairmanship of the Rev. Arthur Joice of the United Presbyterian Church, U.S.A.

In many respects, this volume is a companion work to *Stewardship in Contemporary Theology*, a book of theological lectures published by Association Press in 1960. As was the case in the earlier volume, *Stewardship in Contemporary Life* will be useful for the individual Christian who seeks to improve his own personal stewardship. It will help him to understand God's plan for the world, the Church, and the Christian's place as an individual and as a responsible member of the corporate structures of society. He will learn here to be a better witness to Jesus Christ in the complex relationships of the twentieth century. Local church leaders will find this book useful in adult study classes working on the problems of ethics in modern society. Pastors and stewardship leaders will use

the book for background studies in the annual stewardship
canvass in the local church. Professors of Christian ethics
and practical theology will find here resource material in
theology, social ethics, and church administration.

> T. K. THOMPSON, *Executive Director*
> Department of Stewardship and Benevolence
> National Council of Churches

Part I

MOTIVES
FOR GIVING
IN THE
NEW TESTAMENT

---

by *Theophilus M. Taylor*

Secretary of the General Council of the
United Presbyterian Church, U. S. A.,
New York, New York

1

The Stewardship
of God

THE main corpus of Pauline writings is at least ten or fifteen years earlier than the earliest gospel. However, the written gospels reflect the primitive oral gospel, albeit with some embellishments. This was the seed bed of raw materials upon which the epistolary writers reflected, from which they drew their ethical principles, and upon which they established their rules for Christian conduct. This oral gospel, composed of almost innumerable reports of what Jesus had done and said, was unsystematized. But, as the exponents of the *formgeschichtliche Schule* have so well demonstrated, the various units of the gospel materials were themselves called forth out of the memory of the earliest witnesses by the need to establish Christian behavior under particular circumstances. Professor Martin Dibelius put it this way:

. . . Jews, Gentiles, and proselytes, needed some description and application of what was known about Jesus. The same was also necessary when it was a matter of building up and confirming the churches. . . . Hence we must assume the presence of tradition operative in both the missionary work and the preaching in the course of worship. Finally, the same must have been the case for those who were becoming Christians; they required instruction which made them familiar with their new faith, and with the new life which was required of them. It is obvious that this didactic preaching would have to show how faith and life are determined by the words and works of Jesus.[1]

The Gospels as a Point of Departure

The gospels, therefore, should provide us with a point of departure. There is a certain foundational quality about them which cannot be denied or overlooked. Professor Bultmann expresses it thus:

> The message of Jesus is a presupposition for the theology of the New Testament rather than a part of that theology itself. . . . Christian faith did not exist until there was a Christian kerygma; *i.e.* a kerygma proclaiming Jesus Christ . . . to be God's eschatological act of salvation. He was first so proclaimed in the kerygma of the earliest Church, not in the message of the historical Jesus, even though that Church frequently introduced into its account of Jesus' message, motifs of its own proclamation. . . . But the fact that Jesus had appeared and the message which he had proclaimed were, of course, among its historical presuppositions; and for that reason Jesus' message cannot be omitted from the delineation of New Testament theology.
>
> The synoptic gospels are the source for Jesus' message. . . . Furthermore, throughout the synoptics three strands must be distinguished: old tradition, ideas produced in and by the church, and editorial work of the evangelists.[2]

Now for a word about the structure of these studies. As a frame of reference against which to develop the general topic, "Motives for Giving," it is proposed that we deal seriatim with the stewardship of God, of man, and of the Church. Each of these will begin with a passage from the Pauline *kerygma,* but we shall go to the Gospels as well as to other portions of the New Testament for support. Actually, we shall also be compelled to go to the Hebrew Scriptures for the roots of the stewardship idea, because the New Testament teaching on it is unintelligible apart from this background. The rationale for these first three chapters should become apparent as we progress, and requires no further justification at this point.

One final word of an introductory nature should be said. Stewardship (*oikonomia*), like worship (*leitourgia*) and service (*diakonia*), is a way of looking at, or describing, one's entire way of life, one's total conduct (*anastrophē, anastrephesthai*) as a Christian. Stewardship expresses man's fundamental and continuing response to the grace of God. It cannot properly be considered, then, only as a single aspect of Christian discipleship. It is everything one does as a Christian. Any confinement of the term to lesser compass must be recognized immediately as unbiblical and foreign to the central Judaeo-Christian tradition.

When we speak of "motives for giving," therefore, we are not addressing ourselves in any narrow or exclusive way to motives for the giving of monetary offerings, even though this seems to be the primary connotation of the term for the typical church member today. Rather, we are to deal with those motives which drive a person onward to that complete yielding up of self in service, to which Paul often called attention. For example, "For you know the grace of our Lord Jesus Christ, that though he was rich, yet for your sake he became poor, so that by his poverty you might become rich" (II Corinthians 8:9 RSV).* Keeping up with the Joneses religiously, impressing the public with one's acts of benevolence, and collect-

---

* Unless otherwise indicated in parentheses, all biblical translations used in the first four chapters are those of the author of Part I, Dr. Theophilus M. Taylor.

ing income tax deductions, all of which are recognized as motives for giving operative in "respectable Christian circles" today, will find no place in these discussions. We are after something much more fundamental and deep-seated, something that probes to the roots of Christian commitment. Anything less does not really get at the problem.

Now I am rejoicing in my sufferings for your sakes, and I am making up completely in my flesh what are lacking [*antanapleroun ta usteremata*] of the afflictions of Christ for the sake of his body which is the church. Of it I became a servant [*diakonos*] according to the stewardship of God [*kata tēn oikonomian tou theou*], which was granted to me for you, in order to fulfill the word of God [*hina plepōsai ton logon tou theou*]; the secret [*mustērion*] which has been hidden from both angels and men but is now made plain to his saints. God determined to make known to them the treasure of the glory of this secret among the Gentile-nations, which is; Christ in you, the hope of glory (Colossians 1:24–27).

The Greatest Religious Secret of All Time

The Apostle Paul understood the discovery of the stewardship of God as the unveiling of the greatest religious secret (*mustērion*) of all time. The Graeco-Roman world in which he lived was overrun by a host of competing mystery religions, some of Hellenistic and others of exotic origin. Each of them claimed to reveal to its initiates the secrets of life and of the universe. Beside the newer ones springing up on every side, the old familiar cults of Greek religion had been "modernized" or revamped to conform to the mystery cult pattern. By various successive rites of initiation secret religious knowledge was divulged to their devotees. This secret knowledge was purported to effect the removal of all uncleanness and guilt attaching to one's misdeeds, and to promise immortality beyond the pale of this vale of sorrows which is man's present life. All these cults made similar claims, and people clamored to learn the "mysteries"—the religious secrets.

But the tragic irony of the situation lay in two things: (1) the sheer multitude of the cults, and (2) the pitiful way men flitted from one to another, like drowning persons clutching at every piece of passing flotsam. Men hoped for much and received little. Obviously none of the cults had answers that fully satisfied the quests of men. Plutarch, Greek biographer and moralist (A.D. 46–120), was typical of those who could afford the initiation fees of several. He became in turn an initiate to Apollo, then to the Eleusinian mysteries, and finally to Dionysus.

In the midst of such disillusionment Paul proclaimed with unflinching certainty that the greatest mystery-secret of all time had at last been revealed to men in the person of Jesus the Christ, and that this new insight had burst like a flash of lightning upon a darkened world in the crucifixion and resurrection. To the Corinthian Christians he wrote:

But we are speaking wisdom among initiates, and not a wisdom of this age; nor of the rulers of this age who are doomed. Rather we are speaking God's wisdom in a secret [*mustērion*] which has been hidden. God planned it [*hen proorisen*] before the ages for our glory. None of the rulers of this age knew it, for had they known it, they would not have crucified the Lord of glory (I Corinthians 2:6–8).

The demonic forces ruling this present evil age became enmeshed in their own toils. The trap they had set for the Son of God proved to be their own undoing. Had they known all that was involved, they would never have crucified him.

The Apostle Paul was attributing here to the crucifixion the cause of the Satanic hordes' pained surprise (see also

Galatians 4:3–5; Ephesians 1:20–22; 3:9, 10; Colossians 2:9–10, 13–15) in a way that reminds us of the Evangelists' witness to the surprise of the demons whom Jesus exorcized. "Have you come to destroy us?" (Matthew 1:24// Luke 4:34), or "Have you already arrived ahead of time, to destroy us?" (Matthew 8:29; compare Mark 5:7// Luke 8:28), they cried. In effect, he had taken them by surprise. What they had planned as a resounding defeat backfired. The resurrection was something they had not counted on. The death knell they had planned so carefully for the forces of righteousness turned out to be a victory for God, and their own defeat.

The Nature of God's Stewardship

The secret made plain to God's saints in the crucifixion-resurrection event was in fact nothing less than a revelation of God's stewardship (*he oikonomia tou theou*) since they saw in it a clue to the divine plan—"God's planned economy"—his management of his household affairs.

This idea, first broached by Paul in I Corinthians, becomes in turn the central theme of Ephesians and Colossians. The following passages from Ephesians will be recognized to parallel closely the Colossian passage with which we began:

For he has made known to us the secret [*mustērion*] of his will with all wisdom and prudence, according to his good judgment, which he determined in Christ for a stewardship [*oikonomia*] of the fulness of the times to bring all things to fulfillment in Christ in heaven and on earth (Ephesians 1:8–10) . . .

If indeed you have heard about the stewardship of God's grace which was given me for you, that the secret was made known to me, . . . which was not made known in other generations to the sons of men but is now revealed to his saints, apostles and prophets by the Spirit: that the gentile-nations are fellow-heirs, belonging to the same body, and are partakers of the promise in Christ Jesus through the gospel (3:2–3, 5–6) ... to enlighten all men as to the stewardship of the secret which has been hidden from the ages by God who created all things, so that the manifold wisdom of God may now be made known through the church to the rulers and authorities in heaven (3:9–10).

From these passages in I Corinthians, Ephesians, and Colossians, taken together, a number of things about the stewardship of God may be ascertained. The nouns and verbs are particularly instructive.

• *Nouns.* God's stewardship involves his wisdom (*sophia*) and prudence (*phronēsis*) which differ from the wisdom of this age and its rulers. It is a secret wisdom, hidden from men and angels until its revelation in the crucifixion-resurrection event (I Corinthians 2:6–8). It is a manifold or richly varied wisdom (Ephesians 3:10). God's stewardship involves his will (*thelēma*), his good judgment (*eudokia*). It is a stewardship of the fulfillment of the times (Ephesians 1:10). It is a stewardship of his grace (Ephesians 3:2).

• *Verbs.* God's stewardship has been kept a secret (*mustērion*) through all the ages, but by the crucifixion it has been made known by a revelation (*kata apokalupsin egnōristhē* Ephesians 3:3). It has been revealed (*apekaluphthē*) to the saints (Ephesians 3:5). It is to enlighten all men (*phōtisai pantas*, Ephesians 3:9, c. p. 46 B C D G K L lat sy Mcion). It has to do with God's determining things (*proorizein,* I Corinthians 2:7), his planning (*protithesthai*, Ephesians 1:9), but also with his bringing all things to completion in Christ (*anakephalaiōsasthai ta panta en tō Christō*, Ephesians 1:10), and his determination to make (this) known to his saints (Colossians 1:27), and indeed to all men (Colossians 3:9).

God's stewardship is a plan of redemption for the whole world. It encompasses not only the Jews but the Gentile nations (*ta ethnē*), who "are fellow heirs, belonging to the same body, and are partakers of the promise in Christ Jesus through the gospel" (Ephesians 3:6). How this could be is explained in Ephesians 2:11–22, the essence of which is, "Christ Jesus . . . is our peace, who has made us both [Jews and Gentile] one. He destroyed the animosity which separated us, . . . so that he might create in himself a single new humanity, making peace, and might reconcile both in a single body to God through the cross" (Ephesians 2:14–16). Paul understands the crucifixion in terms of atonement, literally "at-one-ment." Its effect is comparable to the geometric axiom that "things equal to the same thing are equal to each other." Hence, persons who are reconciled to, or are at one with, God in Christ, must by the same token be reconciled to, or be at one, with each other. Putting it simply, a Jew reconciled to God in Christ and a Gentile reconciled to God in Christ are automatically reconciled to one another. Gentiles, therefore, are no longer aliens and transients, but fellow citizens (*sumpolitai*) with the saints and members of God's family (*oikeioi tou theou*, Ephesians 2:19).

But there is something more to be noted, namely, that God's stewardship, once it has been revealed in Christ's death and resurrection, is intended to engender a secondary stewardship in those to whom it has been revealed. In both Ephesians 3:2 and Colossians 1:25, the Apostle understands his stewardship as something given him not for himself, but to him for others (*dotheises [dotheisan] moi eis humas*). It was in keeping with this divinely given stewardship that he became a servant (*diakonos*) in Christ's church, in order that God's word should be brought to fulfillment (Colossians 1:25), or that all things should be brought to fulfillment in Christ, whether in heaven or on earth (Ephesians 1:10).

It is obvious here that God's word (*ho logos tou theou*) and all things (*ta panta*) are not to be understood in contradistinction from each other. The fulfilling of all things constitutes a fulfillment of God's word, just as in the Genesis creation account where it is repeated over and over again, "And God said, . . . And it was so!" This is a fundamental characteristic of God's stewardship. What he plans turns out!

God's stewardship is telescopic, unfolding, ever-enlarging, like an expanding universe! God's saints, those to whom the revelation of God's stewardship has been made, discover in that revelation their own stewardship, which is in turn "to enlighten all men as to their stewardship of the secret [of God's stewardship]" (Ephesians 3:9). In this way the manifold wisdom of God is to be made known through the Church, which is the community of God's stewards, in order that all men may become God's stewards. The reconciled community is a community of stewards.

The Message of Jesus on Stewardship

God's *oikonomia*, his household management, must be seen in its fullness. It is his design or plan for the fulfillment of his eternal purpose as summed up in the hyphenated term: creation-providence-redemption. But it is more than that. It is also creation-providence-redemption itself, because what God plans turns out. Men who learn this greatest secret of all time are drawn into the center of God's creative-redemptive purpose and become his fellow workers (*sunergoi,* I Thessalonians 3:2; I Corinthians 3:9, or *sunergountes,* II Corinthians 6:1). Thus it is through redeemed men, those who have become new creatures in Christ, that God carries forward his total scheme of re-

demption and reconciles the world to himself in Christ (II
Corinthians 5:14–6:1), or brings all things to completion
in Christ (Ephesians 1:10).

Just as all fatherhoods, earthly or otherwise, have their
origin in God's fatherhood (Ephesians 3:14), so all stew-
ardships, earthly or otherwise, take their rise in God's
stewardship. Man knows nothing of stewardship until he
learns something about God's stewardship. Or, putting it
the other way around, man will recognize and understand
his own stewardship in direct proportion as he recognizes
and understands God's stewardship.

In some such way one may summarize the *kerygma* of
the Pauline letters on the subject of stewardship. There is
much in the *kerygma* that is colored by a first-century
cosmology. This is to be expected, for revelation always
takes place in dated terms and in thought concepts that
are common currency at the time. Yet when all mytho-
logical elements have been cleared away, something sub-
stantive still remains. Language and ideas that may seem
to be dated, and even jaded, turn out to be vehicles for
timeless truth. As Paul himself put it, describing revelation
to the individual, "the light of the knowledge of the glory
of God in the face of Christ has flooded our hearts, and
we have this treasure in earthen vessels so that the superla-
tive power may be God's and not ours" (II Corinthians
4:6–7). So it is also in regard to revelation in human language. It, like man, is an "earthen vessel." This is the secret
of incarnation.

Now we must probe back behind this stewardship
kerygma into the message of Jesus upon which, along with
the testimony of his life, the *kerygma* was based. The four
evangelists paint a consistent picture of Jesus' life of
perfect obedience to the will (*thelēma*) or sovereignty
(*basileia*) of God. They saw, particularly in his death, the
radical quality of that obedience, typified in his prayer

of submission in Gethsemane: "Not what I will, but what thou wilt!" (Mark 14:36// Matthew 26:39// Luke 22:42; see John 4:34; 5:30; 6:38; 18:11). It was only natural that the early Christian community should abstract the salutation of this prayer of submission, attributed to Jesus in the earliest tradition, "Abba, Father," and use it as a baptismal formula, signifying the believer's submission to the will of God (see Galatians 4:6; Romans 8:15).[3] Thus the believer made formal recognition of God's stewardship—his will and purpose, plan of accomplishment, and *modus operandi* all rolled into one, and made himself one with it.

Stewardship (*oikonomia*) and steward (*oikonomos*) are not dominant terms in Jesus' synoptic vocabulary. They occur only in Luke, in Chapters 12 and 16 (Luke 12:42; 16:1, 2, 3, 4, 8; see also *oikonomein,* to be, or serve as, a steward, Luke 16:2).

The idea of stewardship, the responsible management of family or household affairs, however, is very common in the Gospels, and surely goes back to the teaching of Jesus. It is too deeply imbedded in the parables not to have had its origin there. The well-known parables of the talents and pounds (Matthew 25:14–30; Luke 19:11–28), which are certainly stewardship parables, are only part of a larger and more dominant theme running through the parables of Jesus, namely: "the motif of an absentee master" (Mark 12:1–12// Matthew 21:33–46// Luke 20:9–19; Mark 13:34–36// Matthew 25:14; Matthew 24:45–51// Luke 12:41–46; Matthew 25:14–30// Luke 19:11–28), to which Professor Cadbury called attention in his 1946 Shaffer Lectures. Speaking of this motif he wrote:

It is easy to see its congeniality to the early church. They were living in precisely such circumstances—awaiting the Lord's return. . . .

. . . The whole setting of an absentee master is integral to these stories and, if the parables go back to Jesus, that feature

goes back too. In that case we have an unexpected disclosure
of his viewpoint. Instead of the comforting presence of God
he seems to teach the absence of God. . . . For long intervals
we have no contact with the one to whom we are responsible.
He is in a distant country and there is no certainty that he
will return soon. Our business is to live as we should live, but
without him. Normal rectitude, fidelity, diligence, are expected
of us and not emergency behavior. "Blessed is the servant
whom his master, when he cometh, shall find so doing." [4]

Besides these absentee landlord parables there are those
of the "wicked steward" (Luke 16:1-9), the "unprofitable
servants" (Luke 17:7-10), the "unmerciful servant" (Matthew 18:23-35), the "laborers in the vineyard" (Matthew
20:1-16), the "unlike sons" (Matthew 21:28-32), and the
"tribute money" (Mark 12:13-17// Matthew 22:15-22//
Luke 20:20-26), each of which deals with some aspect of
stewardship. We may conclude, therefore, that while the
terms for steward and stewardship are not common in the
teaching of Jesus, his message is shot through with the idea
of stewardship!

As a matter of fact, when understood in this way, the
portrait of Jesus preserved in the Gospels is a picture of
one who from the beginning of his conscious life recognized his own stewardship, and the divine source of it.
"Did you not know," he says to Mary and Joseph, "that I
must be concerned with the affairs of my Father?" (Luke
2:49). His public ministry indicates that he was fulfilling
the role given man from creation, "fill the earth and subdue it, rule over . . . every living thing that moves on the
earth" (Genesis 1:28). Taking the earliest gospel as an
example, we find that he teaches with authority and not
like the scribes (Mark 1:22), he exorcizes unclean spirits
with authority, and they obey him (1:27), he heals the
sick (1:31, 34), he cleanses lepers (1:41, 42), he forgives
sins (2:10, 11), he raises the dead (5:39-42), he rules over

nature (4:36–41; 6:45–52). He avoids waste (6:42–44; 8:8, 19, 20). He detests the perversity of those who misrepresent God's will and commands (7:1–13) and points man to the stewardship of the thoughts of his own heart (Hebrew, *lēb;* Greek, *nous;* Mark 7:14–23).

He lets nothing deter him from following where God's will leads him (Mark 8:31–33; 9:30–31; 10:23–34), and expects his disciples to do likewise (8:34–38). Nothing can stand in the way of obedience to God's will (10:17–31). The theme and essence of his life and ministry is summed up thus: "The son of man also came not to be served [*diakonēthēnai*] but to serve [*diakonēsai*] and to give his life a ransom for many" (10:45). He sums up the purpose of man's life in terms of love for God and neighbor (12:28–34), and teaches that intention or motive behind the action is the important consideration in stewardship (12:41–44). He balances his concern over waste with an acknowledgment that there are times for justifiable extravagance (14:3–9). Obedience to the will of God is paramount, even taking precedence over the preservation of life itself (14:36).

Stewardship as Taught by the Torah

It must be recognized that both Jesus and Paul base their understanding of stewardship upon the Torah. In the Hebrew tradition, man was recognized from the very beginning as a steward, or caretaker, of God's good earth. In the more primitive creation account, "God took the man [he had formed and into whom he had breathed life] and put him in the garden of Eden to till it and keep it" (Genesis 2:7, 15). In the later account man is ordered by his maker to "subdue" the earth, and "rule" it (Genesis 1:27, 28). This was one of the most fundamental concepts of Jewish tradition which passed over naturally into Christianity as part of its inheritance from Judaism.

We must begin, therefore, with the affirmation of the Psalmist: "The earth is the Lord's and the fulness thereof, the world and those who dwell therein; for he has founded it upon the seas, and established it upon the rivers" (Psalms 24:1, 2, RSV). God, himself, is the landowner who puts man in the garden to tend it. The motif of the "absentee master" is as ancient as that! Jesus did not dream it up. He simply called attention to it. The gardener is responsible to the landowner. His stewardship is secondary to the stewardship of the owner who knows what he wants done and gives the orders to his steward. The stewardship of God, therefore, is fundamental and implied from the very start.

But, how did Jesus understand the stewardship of God? We should have to reply first of all that he understood it in terms of the fatherhood of God. It was primarily the stewardship of an intelligent and responsible parent rather than that of a landowner or person of means. He thought of it not so much in terms of material possessions but in terms of life and personality. It is familial and relational rather than individualistic and abstract. It involves God's role as Creator-Sustainer-Redeemer. Both Professor Kantonen [5] and Dr. Helge Brattgård have recognized this. The latter writes:

> . . . To be God's *oikonomos* implies a father-child relationship. The "house" in which stewardship takes place is the Father's house. . . . We can say that stewardship is a family concern.[6]

Jesus' conception of the divine stewardship is best seen in the parable of the prodigal son and his elder brother (Luke 15:11–32). It is obvious from this parable that possessions are considered to be secondary, and that the lives of the children are paramount in the father's considerations. As a responsible parent who recognizes his stewardship over the lives of his children and his responsibility to see that they attain personal maturity, the father in the parable makes full allowance for the freedom of his children to respond to him in their own way and according to their own timing. He shows equal patience with the son who breaks all the rules and the one who lives carefully by the family rules. Both sons have childish outlooks which require maturing. Though he could have refused the younger son's request, he did not, because he hoped he would eventually reach the right decision for himself without prompting or pressure of any kind. He could have withdrawn his favor from his elder son for his ungracious attitude toward his profligate brother, but he did not, for he wanted him to learn how to rejoice at the repentance of the wrongdoer and welcome him back into the family. The attitude toward things—material possessions—is rectified when men's relationships toward God and toward one another are rectified. They are to be used for the redemption of persons.

Paul makes precisely the same point in Romans. The seemingly chaotic state of things falls back into orderliness when men assume their true natures as "sons of God" or "new creatures in Christ."

Creation anticipates with eager longing the revelation of the sons of God [new creatures in Christ, II Corinthians 5:17], for creation was subjected to meaningless futility not by its own desire, but by the one who subjected it hopefully, because creation itself will be set free from the slavery of corruption to the glorious freedom of the children of God. For we know that the whole creation is groaning in travail to the present moment; and not only so, but we ourselves who possess the first fruit of the Spirit groan within ourselves anticipating adoption, the redemption of our bodies (Romans 8:19–23).

The entire creation is here personified as agonizing in childbirth, under the curse which was incurred by the fall of man. The curse was brought on by man's failure to assume a responsible stewardship of the creation over which God had set him in charge. As in the parable of the prodigal, God's stewardship makes allowance for the freedom of man to respond when and how he may determine. As the prodigal at last came to his senses and determined to return to his father, so men will one day return to their senses and acknowledge God as their heavenly Father. Though he could do so, and indeed, as Creator-Father-God, is entitled to do so, he does not crack the whip and make men jump to do his bidding. Rather, he waits with outstretched arms for the prodigal to return of his own free will. And this he does "in hope," confident of the outcome because, to use the Pauline phrase, he is in Christ reconciling the world to himself. And the Christian, possessing the first fruit of the Spirit, like creation, yearns for the redemption of the physical part of his own nature, his body.

The canonical evangelists agree that the heart and core of Jesus' teaching concerned the sovereignty (kingdom) of God (*hē basileia tou theou*).[7] Moreover, it is easy to see that although he used a number of figures or analogies by which to explain that sovereignty, the one which he relies on more than any other is that of the Semitic patriarchal family. There are numerous references to "your Father who is in heaven" (Mark 11:25; Matthew 5:16, 45; 6:1, 14, 26, 32, et cetera). He teaches his disciples to address God as "Our Father" (Matthew 6:9// Luke 11:2), and declares that those "who do the will of God" are his brothers, sisters, and mother (Mark 3:31–33). Those who are disinherited by their own flesh and blood because they have chosen to follow Jesus are assured that they will be repaid "a hundredfold now in this time [through their entry into God's family], houses and brothers and sisters and mothers and children and lands, with persecutions, and in the age to come eternal life" (Mark 10:29f).

God's sovereignty is another way of referring to God's stewardship. Jesus does not call his followers to an abstract stewardship of things but to the stewardship which is expected of a member of a Semitic patriarchal family where, as there is a joint or shared ownership, there is also a joint or shared responsibility. The members of the family have their rights only as they have respected the rights and authority of the Father. The absolutely fundamental character of the Father's stewardship or sovereignty for that of any member of the family, or for the whole family, is assumed at all times. It is "the sovereignty [kingdom] of God" that is regulative for all men who understand their true, God-given nature. Their stewardship has meaning only in its relationship to, or in the context of, the stewardship of God.

The Influence of the Greek World

The influence of the Hellenic world upon the early Christian Church only served to enforce this particular notion that was already indigenous to the Judaic tradition out of which the Church was born, namely, that man lives in a purposeful world or universe and is constrained to conform to it. Upon this point Jews and Greeks agreed, even though they arrived at the conclusion from diametrically opposite directions in logic. Men like Philo-Judaeus of Alexandria saw in this agreement more than a mere fortuity.

The Jew, reasoning from the analogy of his own being as a person, assumed a personal God from the beginning. This is essentially why the Torah and the Hebrew Scriptures begin as they do: "In the beginning, God. . . ." From that point the Jew reasons forward through what the theologian refers to as God's works of creation, providence, and redemption, to the world as he knows it (ha 'eretz).

God is not only personal: he was thought of by virtually all Semites as the patriarchal father of his people, ancestor of the family and tribe. For the writers of the Hebrew Scriptures, then, to deal with the Source, Origin, or Creator of the earth and its inhabitants in terms of fatherhood was perfectly natural. (See Hosea 1:10, 11; Isaiah 1:2 and 9:6; Jeremiah 3:4, 19 and 31:9; Deut.-Isaiah 63:16; 64:8; 65:1ff; II Samuel 7:14; Deuteronomy 1:31; 8:5; 32:6, 18.) God was immanent, always closely allied with the affairs of his people. The earth (ha 'eretz) is God's good creation placed at man's disposal, and over which man created in God's image was appointed caretaker or steward. Thus it is man's willful disobedience, his prostitution of God's good gifts for his own selfish ends, that places creation, the good earth, under a curse (Genesis 3:14–19). Only, therefore, through man's redemption and his recovery of the image of God which he has marred by his sin, is there hope for creation (Romans 8:18–25).

The Greek, on the other hand, reasoned in precisely the opposite direction. He began with his environment, the natural world (kosmos phuseos) in which he found himself. In this world he perceived an ordered system, which bears a rough relation to the Jewish concept of the basically "good earth." He recognized in this ordered system certain laws of nature (nomoi phusikoi) which, given the same set of circumstances, were observed always to operate in the same way. Therefore, his name for this kind of world was cosmos, which literally means "order," as over against chaos, "disorder." From the ordered system he reasoned backward to a divine Mind (nous) which had brought it into being. Since his universe was rational he saw it as the product of divine Reason (logos). Man was recognized as the highest form of life in the universe. His reasoning faculty set him above all other forms of life, and this reasoning faculty was looked upon as a spark of the divine Reason (*logos*) planted within man. This was man's mind (*nous*).

This kind of reasoning typified the reflections of educated men in the Golden Age of Greece. The old polytheism of Homer and Hesiod was gone. The probing, embarrassing questions of the early Ionic philosophers about the numerous deities and their questionable conduct in traditional mythology had started the process. It only remained for Socrates, Plato, and Aristotle to finish the job. The old myths, therefore, had to be reinterpreted; and the gods and goddesses were thereby transmuted into functions or manifestations of the one divine Principle. Monotheism was accepted among intellectuals, but disillusionment with the ancient anthropomorphic deities kept the Greeks from settling for a personal concept of God. The deity was an abstract, mechanical Mind or Reason. In this kind of world man, a microcosm, lives benignly when he observes the laws of nature and brings himself into conformity with the macrocosm.

From the very beginning of the Christian movement, Christians have been indebted to both world views. They have informed each other in such a way that it is often difficult to disentangle the strands. All the writers of the New Testament, but notably Paul and the authors of Hebrews and the Fourth Gospel, have been under the influence of both, chiefly because they had something in common which is essential to useful, meaningful life. Both these classical world views posit a world of order and behind it a reasoning, purposeful Being who has a plan for his creation, his people—for all mankind. The step from an orderly world to a moral universe is a very short one. If there is order or system, anything that distorts or perverts it, whatever deters its orderly operation, or postpones the realization of its intention, becomes immoral and is opposed to orderliness, right or proper conduct. In man's discovery of an ordered world and universe he has found meaning outside himself and he knows henceforth that if his own life is to have meaning, it must be found within the framework of, and in the form of a contribution to, that larger universal meaningfulness.

This, in essence, is the fundamental notion of Jesus with regard to stewardship. There is a stewardship of God which man should recognize. In Jesus' terminology, this is "the sovereignty [kingdom] of God" into which Jesus bade men to enter. God's sovereignty-stewardship is recognized and entered by those who do the will of their Father who is in heaven, no matter what the consequences may be. Jesus himself set the example for this perfect kind of stewardship by his voluntary obedience to death, even death on a cross (Philippians 2:8), and expects similar voluntary obedience on the part of his followers (Mark 8:34–37// Luke 9:23–27// Matthew 16:24–26; Luke 9:51–62; compare Matthew 8:18–22). It is fundamentally a stewardship of life rather than of things or possessions, save that these must be used by man in his stewardship of life as God intends them to be used.

So far as "motives for giving" are concerned, we are bound to note that there is no coercion involved. Man must see the reasonableness of his doing the will of God, the folly of following his own unregenerate inclinations any longer and, like the prodigal, must come to his senses and say to himself, "I will arise and go to my father, and . . . will say to him, 'Make me as one of your hired servants'" (Luke 15:18, 19). Man's obedience, his willingness to bring himself into conformity with the will (sovereignty) of God, is both rational and voluntary.

Man's primary motivation, therefore, for giving of himself or of his possessions, which in the Semitic mind were treated as mere extensions of the self or soul,[8] springs from a proper self-understanding. This involves his acknowledgment that he himself is part of God's "good creation," and therefore owes his very existence to God. It involves his recognition that God has endowed him with a reasoning faculty that sets him off apart from and above all other forms of creation, and that in this respect at least he has been made in God's image. It involves his understanding that because he possesses this reasoning faculty, he has been placed in a position of responsible stewardship over the good gifts of creation. He has been able to discern a divine purpose permeating the entire creation, God's ordered system. But it also involves man's frank recognition, first, of his own inadequacies, the admission that he continually does what he knows he should not do and neglects what he knows he should do, and, second, of God's all-sufficiency, the admission that God "has demonstrated and confirmed [*sunistanai*] his love for [man] in that while we were still sinners Christ died for us" (Romans 5:8).

This places man under a double moral obligation. Not only does he owe his existence to God as Creator. He also owes his redemption, his salvation from himself, to God as Redeemer in Jesus Christ. "[We] are not [our] own, [we] have been bought at a price" (I Corinthians 6:19; compare 7:23). Therefore, a man is under moral obligation to "glorify God with [his] body," and with all that he is and has at his disposal. Yet, in spite of all this, man still acts with freedom, for the obligation is moral and not mandatory. Accepting the gracious act of God in Jesus Christ should bring a gracious response upon man's part. It is this for which our heavenly Father hopes, when we come to our senses amidst the husks in the far country, and he waits with open arms to receive us when at last we do just that.

NOTES FOR CHAPTER 1

1. *From Tradition to Gospel* (New York: Charles Scribner's Sons, 1935), p. 14. By permission.
2. Rudolf Bultmann, *Theology of the New Testament* (New York: Charles Scribner's Sons, 1951), Vol. I, p. 3. By permission.
3. See T. M. Taylor's article, " 'Abba Father' and Baptism," in *Scottish Journal of Theology*, Vol. 11, No. 1, pp. 62–71.
4. H. J. Cadbury, *Jesus: What Manner of Man* (New York: The Macmillan Company, 1947), pp. 43–45. See context, pp. 42–54.
5. T. A. Kantonen, *A Theology for Christian Stewardship* (Philadelphia: The Westminster Press, 1956).
6. Dr. Helge Brattgård, *God's Stewards* (Minneapolis: Augsburg Publishing House, 1963), p. 82.
7. *Cf.* T. M. Taylor, "Kingdom, Family, Temple, and Body," in *Interpretation*, Vol. XII, No. 2, 1958, pp. 181–183.
8. *E.g.*, see Johannes Pedersen, *Israel: Its Life and Culture* (London: Oxford University Press, 1926, 1946), Vol. I, pp. 170, 228f.

QUESTIONS FOR DISCUSSION

1. What motives did Paul use in fund raising?
2. In what way is it wrong to speak of God's stewardship? In what way is it right?
3. Is it presumptuous to say that God's hidden plan of the ages has been revealed in Jesus Christ?

2

The Stewardship
of Man

As many, therefore, as are led by God's Spirit, these are God's sons, for you did not receive a spirit of slavery [when you were baptized] that you should again fear, but you received a Spirit of adoption, by which we cry, "Abba, Father." The Spirit himself testifies with our spirits that we are God's children. And if [we are] children, [we are] also heirs, heirs indeed of God and fellow-heirs of Christ, if indeed we suffer with him, in order that we may also be glorified with him (Romans 8:14–17).

The Root of Man's Stewardship

We have seen that the stewardship of God is the root of man's stewardship, and the place where any understanding of stewardship on his part must begin. Though in the passage from Romans, quoted above, the Apostle Paul does not employ the term stewardship, or any of its cognates, its bearing upon the problem of man's stewardship is fundamental. Man's stewardship is rooted in his being a son of God, and as such an heir in the household and a fellow heir with Jesus Christ, God's unique Son through whom he is reconciling an estranged world to himself. The point is that the man who knows himself to be a son of God accepts the overarching purpose of his heavenly Father and conforms himself to it. He has a personal stewardship of his own life and possessions within the larger, comprehensive stewardship of God. His personal stewardship, moreover, is not that of an outsider, a stranger to the house, nor even of a paid employee. Rather, it is the stewardship of a son, a member of the family, and a proper heir to the family holdings.

But how does man come to the knowledge that he is a son of God? That is the real question which Paul is seeking to explain here in Romans. Both Jesus and Paul accepted the Old Testament *kerygma* that the earth and all its inhabitants were God's by right of creation. They also accepted without question the teaching of the natural fatherhood of God as found in the creation accounts and the prophetic writings of the Old Testament (for example, compare Genesis 1:26, 27 with 5:3; Isaiah 64:8; Malachi 2:10), and which was later enshrined in the Lucan genealogy of Jesus (Luke 3:23–38). This is certainly implied in the parable of the prodigal son. And they were also agreed that the seriousness of man's estrangement from God, his heavenly Father, was such that some dramatically decisive act on man's part was required both to signal and inaugurate his return to a rightful place within God's family. But it is not so certain whether they were fully agreed as to the nature of that dramatically decisive act.

That Christian baptism must ultimately be traced to the baptism of John is a point with which few will quarrel. The testimony of the Gospels, Acts, and the Epistles, all apparently points in this direction. However, the position which baptism held in the teaching and ministry of Jesus himself is uncertain. Though there can be little doubt of the accuracy of the report of all three synoptic evangelists that Jesus was himself baptized by John (Mark 1:9; Matthew 3:13–15; Luke 3:21), and that the early Church understood he had commanded baptism after the resurrection (Matthew 28:19, 20; Acts 1:4, 5; 2:38), there are no synoptic references to the practice having a place in his earthly ministry. In the Fourth Gospel there is a strange reference to Jesus' being aware that the Pharisees had heard he was baptizing more disciples than John, but the evangelist immediately follows this statement with the explanation, "However, Jesus himself did not baptize, but his disciples [did]" (John 4:1, 2).

It would appear from the Gospels, therefore, that Jesus neither practiced nor taught baptism as an integral element in his own public ministry. When he sent the twelve out on tour he told them to preach, "The kingdom of heaven is at hand" (Matthew 10:7); and Mark reports that "they went out and preached that men should repent" (Mark 6:1). They were to "heal the sick, raise the dead, cleanse lepers, [and] cast out demons," but there are no instructions to baptize! From Mark's summary of Jesus' own message: "The time is fulfilled, and the kingdom of God is at hand; repent and believe the Good News" (Mark 1:15// Matthew 4:17), and from the report that this was also in essence John's message (Mark 1:4// Matthew 3:2// Luke 3:3), we may reasonably assume that Jesus issued a simple call to repentance (*metanoein, metanoia,* see Matthew 11:20, 21 and 12:41; Luke 13:3; 15:7).

Becoming a Member of God's Family by Repentance

Repentance (*shūv, metanoein, metanoia*) was from its roots in Judaism a dramatically decisive act in itself. The Hebrew word *shūv* meant a reversal, a right-about-face. The Greek word *metanoia,* though not quite so dramatic, meant an abrupt change of mind and, hence, a change of course or action. In the biblical context it always indicates the decisive change that takes place when man says "No" to self, and "Yes" to God—"Not my will, but thine be done." Repentance is the fundamental thing, the change itself, rather than any outward sign of that change. So far as Jesus was concerned it would seem that repentance was the dramatically decisive act required by the seriousness of man's estrangement from God if he was to recover his filial place and responsibilities in God's household. This is wholly consistent with Jesus' habit of cutting back to essentials. It is by this act that man acknowledges "the sovereignty [kingdom] of God," becomes a member of God's family (Mark 3:35// Matthew 12:50) and, as such, a responsible steward in God's house, doing the Father's will (Matthew 21:28–32). Moreover, Jesus teaches that when this decisive step has been taken there can be no turning back (Luke 9:62).

Entering the Kingdom of God by Baptism or Adoption

Whether Jesus either taught or practiced baptism, he accepted it at John's hands. Very soon after the crucifixion, baptism was accepted in the early Christian community as the dramatically decisive public act by which a person was introduced into the sovereignty (kingdom) of God. According to Acts men were invited to be baptized from the day of Pentecost onward (Acts 2:38, 41; 8:12, 16, 38, et cetera), and Paul was among them (Acts 9:17–18). Certainly Paul accepts baptism as a part of the tradition he has received (I Corinthians 1:13–17; 12:13; Galatians 3:27), and evidently on occasion he himself administered the rite (I Corinthians 1:14–16).

For Paul, baptism is primarily the rite of incorporation into the body of Christ and of participation in the one Spirit of God (I Corinthians 12:13); but it is also the rite of adoption (*huiothesia;* see also Galatians 3:26–4:7; Romans 8:9–17; Ephesians 1:5)! It is peculiarly in this rite that a man may come to the knowledge that he is a son of God. This is spelled out in the passage from Romans 8 with which we began this chapter. In baptism, Paul has said, "all were made to drink of the same Spirit" (I Corinthians 12:13); and here we learn that those who are led by God's Spirit are his sons. This is "the Spirit of adoption," he said, "by which [when we are baptized] we cry, Abba, Father" (as Jesus did in Gethsemane, "Not what I will, but what thou wilt," Mark 14:36).

Paul himself may be the first to interpret Christian baptism into Christ's name as adoption. At least there is no earlier evidence. Judaism had no common practice of formal adoption proceedings. Both Greeks and Romans, however, observed the practice, and *huiothesia* was a very common term in Hellenistic inscriptions from the second century B.C. onward, particularly in the expression "by adoption" (*kath huiothesian*). Either Paul or Christians before him saw in adoption a meaningful symbol of Christian baptism. Legal adoption proceedings involved formal declarations in the presence of witnesses on the parts both of the person adopting and of the one being adopted. This is reflected in Galatians 3:26–4:7 as well as in Romans 8:14–17.

In the earlier Galatian passage Paul seems to have in mind two possible situations: one in which a slave was manumitted and then adopted by his former master, and another in which a slave freed by one master was adopted by another. According to the latter, Christians were, prior to their baptism (namely, adoption), "enslaved to the elemental spirits of the universe" (Galatians 4:3); but, according to the former, "God sent out his Son . . . to redeem [Greek: *exagorazein,* literally 'to buy up,' or 'buy back'] those who were under the law [and thus enslaved] so that [they] might receive their adoption" (Galatians 4:4-5).

Actually, however, neither the adoption of a freed slave by his former master, nor the adoption by one master of a slave freed by another, quite fits the situation. For, as J. B. Lightfoot pointed out more than half a century ago, "Potentially indeed men were sons before Christ's coming (verse 1)," [1] and we might add they were sons before their baptisms. In this connection it is probable that Paul intended by the *exagorazein* of verse 5 the meaning "to buy back." In other words, he is thinking closely along the lines implied in Jesus' parable of the prodigal. Man is a son all along—even while he is wasting his substance in a strange land, and even though his return, because of the depths of his dereliction, requires to be signalized by a dramatically decisive act. The very basis for the possibility of his restoration lies in his being a son all along. His behavior, heinous and despicable as it was, cannot erase the fact that he bears the image and likeness of his father. The prodigal, who came to his senses in a far country and acknowledged that even his father's servants were better off than he now was, determined to ask his father to take him back as a hired servant. We must note, however, that the father refused, receiving him back into the family as a son with no questions asked.

But, as we have suggested above, it was probably the formal declarations made by the person proposing to adopt a son, and by the person being adopted, that commended the legal adoption procedure to Paul as a way of viewing the significance of Christian baptism. In essence, the person adopting calls the one to be adopted, "Son!", and the person being adopted calls the one adopting him, "Father!" Thus Paul can write to the Romans, "As many . . . as are led by God's Spirit, these are God's sons, for . . . [when you were baptized] . . . you received a Spirit of adoption, by

which we cry, 'Abba, Father'" (Romans 8:14, 15). In
Galatians he writes, "Because you are sons, God sent out
the Spirit of his Son into our hearts, crying, 'Abba, Father'
[just as his Son did]. So you are no longer a slave but a
son, and if a son then an heir through God" (Galatians
4:6, 7). The Spirit of God, the Spirit of his Son, and the
Spirit of adoption are obviously one. "The Spirit himself
testifies with our spirits that we are God's children and if
children then heirs, heirs indeed of God, and fellow heirs
with Christ" (Romans 8:16, 17). In baptism Paul says that
God's Spirit testifies with our spirits that we are God's sons
and, in turn, the Spirit of adoption, God's Spirit, enables
us to say, "Abba, Father!"

The parallel in the parable of the prodigal is that when
the son returns home he says, "Father, I have sinned
against heaven and before you, I am no longer worthy to
be called your son" (Luke 15:21). But his father said to
his servants—that is, witnesses—"Bring the best robe, . . . a
ring, shoes, . . . the fatted calf, . . . for this my son was
dead and lives again, he was lost and has been found"
(Luke 15:22–24). The prodigal acknowledges his father
once more, which implies his return to the family and submission to the father's will; and the father acknowledges
his son once more before witnesses, implying the repent-
ant prodigal's bona fide reception into the family circle.

"Abba, Father" must therefore be recognized as liturgical shorthand for "Not what I will, but what thou wilt"
(Mark 14:36). It marks the believer's submission to the
will or sovereignty (kingdom) of God, and was undoubtedly widely used as a response of the believer immediately
following his baptism.[2] Since the gift of the Spirit was the
normally expected accompaniment of baptism in the earliest Christian community (I Corinthians 12:12–13; Galatians 3:27–4:7; compare the exceptions to the rule which
are noted in Acts 8:14–16; 10:44–48; 19:1–7), it was only

after the reception of the Spirit that the new believer could say, "Abba, Father."

For the first time in his life the person just baptized would be empowered and entitled to say, *Abba, ho Pater* (Gal. 4:6; Rom. 8:15). Just as Paul had declared that "no one, speaking in the Spirit of God says, 'Jesus is anathema,' neither can any one say, 'Jesus is Lord,' excepting by the Holy Spirit" (I Cor. 12:3), so here, no one can rightfully say, *Abba, ho Pater* unless it be in the power of the Spirit (Gal. 4:6; Rom. 8:14–16). . . .[3]

All this thought in Paul is consonant with the teaching of Jesus upon what constitutes membership in the family of God or entrance into his sovereignty (kingdom). "Not everyone who says to me, 'Lord, Lord,' shall enter the kingdom of heaven, but he who does the will of my Father who is in heaven" (Matthew 7:21). "Whoever does the will of God, this is my brother, and sister, and mother" (Mark 3:35). In his parable of the unlike sons, Jesus hammers the same truth home:

A man had two sons. Coming to the first he said, "Son, go work today in my vineyard." And he answered, "Yes, Sir," but he did not go. Coming to the second he said the same thing, and he answered, "I will not," but later having repented he went. Which one of the two did his father's will? They said, "The second one." Jesus said to them, "Truly I say to you, Tax collectors and prostitutes are entering into the sovereignty [kingdom] of God. For John came to you in the way of righteousness and you didn't believe him, but the tax-collectors and prostitutes believed him, and when you saw it you did not repent and believe him" (Matthew 21:28–32).

"Doing the Father's will" in Jesus' message means the same thing as being "led by the Spirit of God" in Paul's message. Both are indicative that the persons of whom these things are said are members of God's family or household and as such are subject to his economy or stewardship. Thus we see that *thelēma, basileia,* and *oikonomia* are virtually synonymous, and that what is said of one may also be said of the others. Each of these terms represents a different way of speaking of God's plan for creation—for man and the world; and it is a plan with which a reasoning being may ultimately be expected to conform voluntarily.

It is a relatively easy thing to say that a man becomes a son or child of God when he does the Father's will and is led by his Spirit. For the questions may then be raised: What is the will of God? and, How is one led by God's Spirit? It has been relatively simple to establish the broad outlines of God's plan, his *oikonomia* or stewardship—that it is a plan to reconcile the world to himself, to bring all things to completion, to sum up all things, in Christ. We have seen that it is the single continuum of God's purpose as expressed in the *Heilsgeschichte* of creation-providence-redemption.

But what does this mean for the individual who seeks to be a member of God's family and to act within his sovereignty? In his day-to-day life how does he do God's will? How is he led by God's Spirit? How does he do the work of a steward in God's house? How does he assure himself that his own stewardship contributes to the larger stewardship of God?

Steward of the Household

The use of the terms steward, stewardship, as we have seen, are not frequent in the Gospels; but the idea of stewardship permeates the message of Jesus, particularly in the large number of parables which follow the theme of an absentee landowner or master who expects or demands an accounting upon his return. Our first obligation, therefore, is to see what is involved in the idea of stewardship as it is used in the Gospels and in the Graeco-Roman world of the first century. The idea has both a Semitic and

a Hellenistic history, and it is of more than passing interest
that both histories arise from a pastoral setting. In the
patriarchal tradition of the Old Testament the idea first
occurs in Genesis 15:2, 3, where Abraham says, "the inheritor [literal Hebrew, 'son of possession'] of my house is
this Damascene, Eliezer. . . . Behold, thou hast given me
no offspring; and a slave born in my house will be my
inheritor." The King James Version may very well have
been justified in rendering *ben meshek* (son of possession)
as steward; for the description given in Genesis 24 of the
slave who was the oldest in Abraham's house, and who
had charge of all he owned was probably understood by
the redactor to be the same person, Eliezer; and this is
certainly the description of a steward. Another phrase
translated steward in the Old Testament is found in the
Joseph narratives (Genesis 43:19; 44:1, 4) "the man who is
over his house [*ha-'ish asher 'al bethi*]," which places the
emphasis upon authority, presumably over members of the
household as well as over possessions, for the phrase "over
his house" certainly carried this connotation. Incidentally
it is this phrase which the author of the Epistle to the
Hebrews picks up out of its literalistic Septuagint translation, and applies to Jesus. "Moses [like Eliezer] was in
[God's] house [*en holo to oiko autou*] as a servant, . . . but
Christ was over his house [*e ai ton oikon autou*] as a Son,
whose house we ourselves constitute, if we hold fast our
boldness and boasting of hope" (Hebrews 3:5–6). This
emphasizes the paternal and familial character of stewardship to which we pointed in the first chapter. It is a stewardship of life and of lives primarily and only secondarily
a stewardship of material possessions, for people (Old
Testament; *nephāshōth,* souls) are always more important
than things (*debārim*). Things take whatever importance
they may have from their association with persons or souls.
Hence we may say that the Old Testament concept of the

steward was that of a servant whom the master placed in charge of his household or family and all its possessions. A good example of the intimate nature of responsibilities that were his may be seen in Genesis 24 where Abraham's steward is sent to Mesopotamia to procure a wife for his son, Isaac.

The terms *oikonomos, oikonomia,* and *oikonomein* in Greek usage are derived from *oikos* and *nomas* (plural: *nomades,* literally "nomads"), a pastoral people. Three verbs eventuated from this latter root: (1) *Nomeuein,* to pasture, be a shepherd, tend flocks; (2) *Nemein,* to deal out, dispense, pay out, distribute, manage, direct or operate (as a farm), to hold, or occupy land; and (3) *Nomān,* to deal out, distribute, direct, guide, manage. The pastoral responsibilities of a nomadic people for finding food and forage for the tribe and its flocks and herds, and dispensing it to them, is apparently in the background. Thus the steward in Greek thought is the person responsible for the daily welfare of the family, and this is not just what we of the Western world would define as family. Rather, it comprises the patriarchal joint family which includes at least three generations: father and mother, sons and their wives, unmarried daughters, and grandchildren, not to mention servants, which is still the common pattern in most of Asia and the Near East. The steward is the deputy to whom the patriarch of the joint family leaves all minor details, and who bears rule in his absence. The steward was the provider and dispenser of daily food for the family.

Latin usage in the Western Church of the second and third centuries followed pretty much in the same kind of pattern. Its terms for the steward were: (1) *dispensator,* the one who portioned out food and supplies; (2) *arcarius,* treasurer; (3) *actor,* director, accountant, administrator of public funds; and (4) *villicus,* manager or superintendent of a *villa* or country estate.

All these terms in Hebrew, Greek, and Latin have left their deposit in the Church's use of the terms dealing with stewardship. From Hebrew we get the notions that the steward shares in the family inheritance, is responsible for the conservation and careful management of the family property, and bears authority with the patriarch (*oikodespotēs, paterfamilias*) over members of the family. From both Hebrew and Greek comes the idea of pastoral responsibility for the family's daily welfare, accountability for daily details in household management in line with the father's policies, and sharing in family authority. As might have been expected, Latin usage, although it still bears signs of the rustic origins of stewardship (compare *dispensator* and *villicus*,) reflects the shift to a more highly developed mercantile economy with such terms as *actor* and *arcarius*. For the first time monetary and fiscal terminology appears in the vocabulary of stewardship, and helps to shape the later concept.

The Parables on Stewardship

We must now return to the Gospels to see the roots of the Christian understanding of the stewardship of man, the individual. First, we must recognize that Jesus' teachings, as well as those of Paul and the later Church, apply the analogy of the steward, of whom there was only one to a family in ancient times, to all the members of the family or kingdom of God. Certain elements that characterized pre-Christian usage, therefore, should not, and indeed cannot, be pressed as illuminating the Christian concept without qualification. For example, in patriarchal times the patriarch of the joint family had absolute life and death authority over all members of the joint family, and in his absence this was transferred to the patriarch's steward "who was over his house." The teaching regarding Christian stewardship holds the familial and relational dimension to be determinative rather than the individualistic and abstract. That is to say, Christian stewardship must always be seen in the context and framework of God's whole house or family.

On the other hand, each Christian has individual stewardship responsibilities that are peculiarly his, but they can never be abstracted completely, nor seen separately, from the family setting. Obviously individual Christians, therefore, cannot as individuals possess the absolute authority that the patriarchal father entrusted to his steward on occasion. Yet they share with their Christian brethren and fellow stewards the authority of the family under God the Father.

A good place to begin with the stewardship of man in the Gospels is with the two parables preserved in Luke in which the specific terminology of stewardship is found. The first of these concerns "the faithful and prudent steward" (*ho pistos oikonomos, ho phronimos*) of Luke 12:42–46. Verses 47 and 48 have all the earmarks of being an appendage to the original parable and are omitted for that reason.

Who now is the faithful and prudent steward whom his master will put in charge of his retinue to issue their rations at the proper time? Blessed is that slave whom his master will find doing so when he comes. Truly I tell you he will put him in charge of all his possessions. But should that slave say to himself, "My master postpones his coming," and he begins to beat the servants and maids, and to eat and drink and get drunk, the master of that slave will come on a day when he does not expect him and at an unknown hour, and he will punish him severely and set him apart with the untrustworthy.

We note first of all that this is one of the parables that use the motif of the absent master. Verse 42 sounds a little like the kind of colophon which Luke often employs to introduce a parable or logion (for example, Luke 13:1; 15:1; 16:14; 18:1, 9), but it may very well be integral to the original parable. If so, Jesus here calls attention with a rhetorical question as to what constitutes a "faithful and prudent steward," which he is about to illustrate with a story. This is somewhat the reverse of the rhetorical question used at the end of a parable to point up "the moral" of the story as in the case of the Good Samaritan (Luke 10:36).

The chief function of the *oikonomos* here described is that of providing for the welfare of the master's retinue of servants (*hē therapeia*) while the master and his immediate family are away. It is the pastoral responsibility of supplying the daily needs of the family, or as much of the family as remains. This is what constitutes being " a faithful and prudent steward" in this particular parable. It is an individual responsibility on the part of the steward for the welfare of fellow members of the household. But it all leads into a discussion of a steward who is unfaithful and imprudent and ends up with a warning to such persons.

As in the parables of the unlike sons, the publican and Pharisee at prayer, the houses on rock and sand, we find a contrast in this case between a faithful and prudent steward and one that is unfaithful and imprudent. There are the notes of the responsibility and accountability involved in stewardship and of the definiteness of a day of reckoning. The faithful steward enjoys a life of blessedness, he is *makarios;* and the unfaithful steward who takes advantages of his master's absence is assured of severe punishment (*dichotomein*). The verb really means, "He will cut him in two." The absence of the master, which symbolizes the apparent absence of God, man's heavenly Father, from the human scene, always poses a temptation for man. Like Adam and Eve, he thinks he is unseen and that he can get away with his irresponsible behavior, but Jesus assures him his day of reckoning, of rendering his accounts, will come upon him suddenly and unexpectedly.

Neither Jesus nor Paul (see II Corinthians 5:10; Romans 14:10, and so on) hesitated to appeal to man's fear of a day of reckoning. This is not the best nor the highest motive, certainly, to appeal to in man by way of urging him to a responsible stewardship, but it is one that the New Testament does not avoid. As a matter of fact, the real point of the motif of the absent master or landowner, which plays so large a role in the gospel, is to be found in the absent master's unexpected return and its catastrophic results for those who have been untrustworthy.

Turning now to the second Lucan parable which preserves the specific terminology of stewardship, that of the dishonest steward, Luke 16:1–8, we note that here again certain extraneous logia have been added to the parable itself by the evangelist; but there is little doubt that the original parable ended with verse 8.

There was a certain wealthy man who had a steward, and charges were brought to him that this fellow was squandering his possessions. And when he had summoned him, he said, "What is this I hear about you? Give an account of your stewardship for you can no longer be steward!" The steward then said to himself, "What shall I do, for my master is taking away the stewardship from me? I am not strong enough to dig! I am ashamed to beg! I know what to do so that when I am dismissed from my stewardship they will take me into their houses." And summoning one by one his master's debtors he said to the first one, "How much is your debt to my master?" And he said, "A hundred storage jars of oil." And he said to him, "Take your bills, sit down quickly and write 'Fifty!'" Then he said to another, "How much is your debt?" And he said, "A hundred tons of wheat." And he said to him, "Take your bills and write, 'Eighty.'" The master praised the dishonest steward because he acted prudently [*phronimōs*], for the sons of this age are for their own generation more prudent than the sons of light.

This particular parable has probably gathered to itself more erroneous interpretations than most others, chiefly because it has not been recognized as an *argumentum ad hominem* addressed to persons who, though they may now be disciples, are still thoroughly familiar with, and not yet far removed from, the ways of the unregenerate world—the dog-eat-dog existence of commercial intercourse which has not measurably changed since the first century. Here it is "everyone for himself" with "no holds barred." Financial integrity, business ethics, and personal morality can go by the board when it is a question of "getting ahead in business." This is an excellent example of Jesus' ability to communicate with the man in the street, the man who typified the urban life of the time. He was talking in terms he understood.

The problem of interpretation is raised for Christians, first, because they have assumed that the master in this parable, as in others using the absent-master motif (for example, Mark 12:1–9; 13:32–37), is analogous to God; and, second, this creates an impossible situation in that God apparently praises or commends the unscrupulous behavior of a dishonest steward. It should be noted in this connection that the foregoing assumption, namely, that the master in all the absentee-owner parables represents God, is not a necessary deduction. Jesus does not fall into the trap of making all capitalists (landowners) saints and all laborers (servants, and the like) sinners. All of Jesus' parables are drawn from real life. He recognizes that in the surrounding society of his day many landowners were just as unscrupulous in amassing their landholdings as their stewards were in administering them. Both the master and the steward in this parable take the dog-eat-dog world for granted. This is why the master in the parable, who is certainly not God, admires the shrewd (*phronimōs*) way in which his steward behaves when at an impasse.

The whole story to this point is lifted right out of the common daily experience of the disciples to whom the evangelist says Jesus was addressing himself. Certainly men like Peter and Andrew, James and John, who made their living by marketing the Galilean fish they caught, and Matthew the tax collector, not to mention the others, understood perfectly well what he was talking about. This kind of thing happened every day. It was perfectly natural for a master who was a man of the world himself to recognize the shrewd manipulation of the accounts by a steward who was on the way out anyway, so that he would have friends to come to his aid when he was finally ousted.

But the point Jesus is making comes out clearly only in the last half of verse 8: "For the sons of this age are shrewder [more prudent], for their own generation [that is, on their own terms] than the sons of light." The two phrases: "sons of this age" and "sons of light" are, of course, Semitisms, and as such of pre-Christian origin. It will be recalled, for instance, that in Genesis 15:2, Abraham referred to his steward, Eliezer, as a "son of possession." J. M. Creed wrote in 1930:

As contrasted with this present age of darkness, the age to come may be thought of as "light" and its citizens as "sons of light." The phrase is not found elsewhere in the synoptic Gospels, and according to S.B. (Strack-Billerbeck, *Kommentar zum Neuen Testament aus Talmud und Midrasch*) it is not rabbinic. But cf. Jo. xii. 26: I Thess. V 5: Eph. v 8.

The phrase suits well "the sons of this age: who are concerned to adapt themselves to the men of their own generation. We must not try to find too close an analogy in this case of the "sons of light." [4]

We have since learned that these phrases apparently originated in the Essene community which produced the Dead Sea scrolls. In the *Manual of Discipline* from Cave IV, members of the community are called upon "to love all the sons of light" and "to hate all the sons of darkness," and God is said to have created for man "two spirits" who are called variously "the spirits of truth and perversion," "the spirits of light and darkness," or "the prince of lights," and "the angel of darkness." Another document from the same cave that was preserved substantially complete is now known as *The War of the Sons of Light with the Sons of Darkness,* from its lead sentence.

Much of the Essene terminology, by what process we cannot be sure, became common currency in the early Christian community, and there is no reason to believe that it was not used by Jesus himself. As with the Essenes, "the sons of light" are obviously members of the community, in this case the Christian community or its antecedent community of the disciples of Jesus, that is, those who have entered the kingdom of God. It is just as obvious that "sons of this present age" are those outside the community who have not submitted to God's will or sovereignty or stewardship. Those who have entered the kingdom are already citizens or "sons" of the new age which is coming.

The point Jesus makes at the end of this parable is a very simple but, at the same time, profound observation. It is that unregenerate men of the world on their own terms often outdo the saints in their imaginative ingenuity and patient persistence in attaining their evil ends. Prudence, shrewdness, or cleverness (*phronimos, phronimōs*) is practical wisdom for everyday life. It is not necessarily evil. It is "just plain common sense," even though this may be defined in different ways. Jesus gave implicit instructions to the Twelve as he sent them off on their preaching mis-

sion: "Behold, I am sending you out like sheep in the midst
of wolves. Therefore, become clever [*phronimoi*] as snakes
and sincere [or innocent] as doves" (Matthew 10:15).
Cleverness and sincerity are not mutually exclusive. We
may paraphrase Jesus something like this: "Oh, that my
disciples in their kingdom stewardship were half as clever
and diligent in seeking and accomplishing God's will as
their worldly counterparts enslaved to the powers of darkness are in attaining their malevolent ends!" If the Christian is to gain his ends, let alone maintain his existence in
this kind of world, he must learn to live by his wits and
to carry on his stewardship in prudent ways. There is no
place for a Christian who does not take his personal stewardship responsibilities seriously. They require his full attention and the dedication of all his skills, particularly the
development of trustworthiness, sincerity, and prudence.

Finally, we must now summarize Jesus' other teachings
as they bear upon the stewardship of man. The logical
place to begin, of course, is with his demand that his disciples deny themselves, which is implied by one's submission to the will or sovereignty of God, take up their
individual crosses, and follow him (Mark 8:34// Matthew
16:24// Luke 9:23). This is followed by his assurance
that whoever selfishly wishes to save his life is bound to
lose it, but that whoever loses his life for the sake of Christ
and the gospel is bound to save it (Mark 8:35// Matthew
16:25// Luke 9:24). Out of the religious tradition of his
own people, Jesus epitomizes man's daily stewardship in
terms of wholehearted love for God and for man's neighbor, whoever he may be (Mark 12:28–31// Matthew 22:
34–40// Luke 10:25–28). As Jesus said of the Son of Man,
he did not come to be served but to serve (Mark 10:45//
Matthew 20:28), so he expects those who have submitted
to God's sovereignty to live lives that are outwardly directed—toward God and neighbor, and not inwardly di-

rected toward self. When this takes the form of contributing to the temple treasury or of almsgiving in behalf of
one's fellow men, it is the purity of motive and the honest
intention that are paramount, rather than the size of the
contribution (Mark 12:41–44// Luke 21:1–4; Matthew 6:
2–4). Man's deliberate corruption or perversion of the
commandments which reflect and particularize the divine
will is especially despicable in Jesus' eyes (Mark 7:1–12//
Matthew 15:1–9).

In this connection an important element in man's stewardship is the management and control of his own heart
(Mark 7:14–23// Matthew 15:10–11, 15–20). Here it must
be understood that the heart, for the Semite, represented
not only the seat of the emotions, but also of the intellect
and will. For the Greeks, and for Western Christendom
since the first century, this is the equivalent of the mind.
Rabbinical theology saw in the heart of the man the seat
of "the evil imagination" (*ha-yētzer ha-ra'*, Genesis 3:6–7;
6:5; 8:21, et cetera) which led him on to overt sin. This
Jesus accepted, and he incorporated a petition for deliver-
ance from it in the prayer he taught his disciples, "Deliver
us from the evil [imagination, *tou ponērou*]" (Matthew
6:13).[5] Here he quite frankly says, "From within, out of
men's hearts [minds], evil plans proceed, . . . all these evil
[imaginations, *ta ponēra*] proceed from within, and they
defile the man" (Mark 7:21; Matthew 15:19, 20). This goes
far to explain the new fivefold law enunciated by Jesus in
Matthew 5, each section of which is preceded with the
formula, "You have heard it said from antiquity . . . , but I
say to you," and his insistence upon the intention of the
heart or mind, and not only the overt act, as that which
constitutes an infraction of God's will or law.

From these considerations it is plain that man, God's
steward, is responsible not only for his conduct or behavior, but for his desires, motives, and intentions. He acts

from reason, from acknowledging that the Father's will is better than his own. He acts from a love and loyalty that must be genuine, and which are directed first toward God, and then toward one's neighbor, who may even be one's enemy (Matthew 5:43–48). He acts from a sincere concern for the fulfillment of God's purposes for his people, his family, his kingdom, and for the world of his creation.

NOTES FOR CHAPTER 2

1. J. B. Lightfoot, *Galatians* (London: Macmillan & Co., Ltd., 1902), p. 168. By permission of the publishers.
2. See "'Abba, Father' and Baptism," in *Scottish Journal of Theology*, Vol. 11, No. 1, 1958, pp. 62–71.
3. T. M. Taylor, *loc. cit.*, p. 70. By permission of *Scottish Journal of Theology*, T. F. Torrance, ed.
4. *The Gospel According to St. Luke* (London: Macmillan & Co., Ltd., 1930), p. 204.
5. See "A Commentary on the Lord's Prayer," T. M. Taylor, in *Current Religious Thought*, Vol. XIV, No. 5, 1954, pp. 20f.

QUESTIONS FOR DISCUSSION

1. Only about seventy years' experience of the Christian churches are recorded in the New Testament. What value can be placed on postbiblical church history as a guide to present-day Christians?
2. Does God have a plan for each man on earth?

3

The Stewardship
of the Church

I exhort you, therefore, I who am a prisoner in the Lord, to conduct yourselves worthily of the calling with which you were called, ² with all humility and consideration, with great patience, upholding one another in love, ³ being diligent to guard the unity of the Spirit in the bond of peace. ⁴ There is a single body and one Spirit, just as you were called in one hope of your calling; ⁵ one Lord, one faith, one baptism, ⁶ one God and Father of all, who is over all, throughout all, and in all. ⁷ To each one of you grace was granted according to the measure of the gift of Christ. . . .

¹¹ And he gave the apostles, and the prophets, and the evangelists, and the pastors and teachers: ¹² (1) for the preparation of the saints for the work of service [diakonia]; (2) for the building up of the body of Christ [i.e. the Church, Eph. 1:22, 23], ¹³ Until we all arrive within the unity of our faith and of the secret-knowledge of the son of God to an initiated (or mature) manhood, to the measure of Christ's full maturity, ¹⁴ [This is] so that we may no longer be infants tossed about and carried away by every fresh teaching in the guesswork of men, by trickery for their scheme of deception. ¹⁵ But being truthful in love let us grow up into him in every respect, who is the head, even Christ, ¹⁶ From him the whole body being

logically brought together and bound together by every supporting and active [*kai enegeias* c. p. 46] tie, produces the growth of the body by the measure of each individual part (Ephesians 4:1-7, 11-16).

The concept of man's stewardship, in these first three chapters, is sandwiched in between the stewardship of God and the stewardship of the Church. This is as it should be, for the stewardship of the individual Christian depends upon both. It cannot be abstracted from the other two. Using a geometrical analogy, we may liken the stewardship of man to an ellipse, the two foci of which are God's stewardship and the Church's stewardship. Within this elliptical field he finds the orbit of his own stewardship. The stewardship of the individual is always to be seen in relationship to the corporate stewardship of God and his family, the family with and under God being corporately owner-operator-steward, working consistently and constructively toward the realization of the ultimate end-goal, the fulfillment of God's plan and purpose for creation—the reconciliation of the world or universe to himself.

The "Joint Family" Structure of Israel

This basically biblical way of looking at man's stewardship is dictated by the historical social phenomenon and concept of the Semitic patriarchal "joint family" (*mishpaḥah*) defined by Ludwig Koehler as the "(larger) family, clan (the circle of relatives in which consanguinity is felt)." [1] For it was in terms of the basic unit of society familiar to him that Hebrew man conceived of the relationship between God and his people. William F. Albright put it this way:

The Hebrews, like their nomadic Semitic forefathers, possessed a very keen sense of the relationship between a patriarchal group (clan or family) and its deity, who was therefore an actual member of the clan and could be addressed by a mortal kinsman as "father, brother," and even as "kindred." All the members of the clan were, accordingly, children, brethren, or kinsmen of the god, who was the head of the house (family).[2]

No one has more accurately described the Hebrew patriarchal family than the late Professor Johannes Pedersen of Copenhagen, whose monumental work, *Israel: Its Life and Culture*[3] will stand as a landmark for years to come.

> . . . A father's house is in itself a family, *mishpaḥa,* and a tribe may be so.
> In the family the chief thing is kinship. When the *mishpaḥa* is used as the connecting link between the father's house and the tribe, then it is due to the fact that it presupposes the father's house. . . . The father's house is a community centering about one man, the father of the house. If we take him as our starting point, then his house comprises all who call him father; his family is all who claim community of kin with him; and this also includes the house. . . .[3]
> . . . *Mishpaḥa* are those who are of common flesh and blood, but it signifies more than what is immediately communicated through it; it is the expression of a common character, of a psychic community. Therefore we cannot wonder that the Israelites once in a while, instead of *mishpaḥa,* use the word *hayya,* signifying those related as a community of life. For the family is the source from which life springs, and those who are one in kin have community of life.[4]

Among the Hebrews Yahweh was therefore looked upon as the supreme Father and Patriarch of the people. He was Father to the house of Israel. Man as individual had no existence apart from the father who had begotten him, and he could not maintain his existence apart from the family to which he belonged and of which he was a member.

Hence Malachi could write, "Do we not all have one Father? Has not one God created us?" (Malachi 2:10).

It was upon the *mishpaḥah* structure, therefore, that all social groups of men were patterned. Early Semitic ideas of kingship and kingdom, of priesthood and prophet's role, arose in this way, probably because in early patriarchal times the father of the family (*mishpaḥah*) was, in effect, king, priest, prophet, teacher for the family. Hence, the term father (*ābh*) was until relatively late times applied to the kings, priests, and prophets in Israel, and probably in Canaanite society as well. Throughout the history of the Hebrew people the *mishpaḥah* remained virtually unchanged.

The most natural thing for Jesus, then, as he conceived of the kingdom of God, was to do so in terms of the *mishpaḥah*, the Semitic patriarchal joint family. This kind of family fulfills its role and performs its function in society so long as all the members of the family maintain their psychic unity. The nucleus of this community is the Father. Members of the family are one with him in every conceivable way. They are of one flesh, one body, one blood, bone and marrow, one heart and soul. They are of one desire, one purpose, and one intention. This means that the Father's will (*thelēma*), his sovereignty or rulership (*basileia*), his economy or stewardship (*oikonomia*), his purpose (*proorizein, protithesthai, prothesis*) is that which in daily life binds the family together and enables all its members to function as a single unit.

This is the setting against which we must understand the gospel theme of "the kingdom of God." This is why Jesus teaches his disciples to address God as "Our Father" (for example, Matthew 6:9// Luke 11:2), to think of God as Father (Matthew 5:45; 6:4, 18; 7:11; Mark 11:25; Luke 6:36; 12:32), and does so himself (Matthew 11:25, 26; Luke 10:21; Mark 8:38; John 17:1, 5, 11, 24, 25, et cetera).

This is why he warns men, "Not everyone who says to me, 'Lord, Lord,' shall enter the kingdom of heaven, but the one who is doing the will of my Father who is in heaven" (Matthew 7:21). This is why he counts those who do the will of God his "brother, and sister and mother," namely, his close relatives (Mark 3:31–35//). And this is why he can tell his disciples that when, to the best of their knowledge, they have done everything that has been commanded and hence expected of them, they should still say to themselves, "We are useless slaves, we have done what we were obligated to do" (Luke 17:10). Obedience is expected of every member of the *mishpaḥah,* be he slave or freeborn son.

The individual, therefore, never thinks, speaks, or works in isolation; for he can never separate himself from the family of which he is a member. Every thought, word, and action is qualified and ultimately determined by the fact that he is a member of that particular family.

It is unthinkable for the Hebrew that men should live apart from families. One of the Hebrew psalmists writes:

A Father of orphans and a Defender of widows is God in his
    holy dwelling place [that is, household].
God causes the solitary ones to dwell in families [*bayitha*].
    (Psalms 68:5, 6)

In his Tübingen lectures on "Hebrew Man," Ludwig Koehler describes the situation thus:

It goes without saying that the Hebrew will marry, for that is the natural course of events. The man cleaves to his wife (Gen. 2:24), and the woman longs for the man (Gen. 3:16). It corresponds to the divine ordering of creation: "Be fruitful and multiply and fill the earth" (Gen. 1:28). "Give me children, or else I die," cries Rachel (Gen. 30:1), and even in the New Testament it is stated that the woman shall be saved through her child-bearing, if she continues in faith and love and sanctification with sobriety (I Tim. 2:15), Man and wife and children form the smallest but also most natural community. The Arabs call the bachelor 'azab, "forsaken, lonely." The Old Testament has no word for this at all, so unusual is the idea. Nor is there known the woman who remains single, since the step to marriage always comes here from the man.[5]

The Stewardship of the Family—that is, of the Church

Coming now to the matter of stewardship (*oikonomia*), it will be seen that although each person who has submitted to the sovereignty (kingdom) of God can be said to have a stewardship of his own, that stewardship cannot be conceived of apart from the stewardship of the entire family.

Quite frankly the stewardship of the Church, if we properly understand it, is the stewardship of a family-operated business in which all have a stake in its success. All members of the family are investors, stockholders, employees, and to some extent managers or members of the board. That is, they must share in the responsible decisions which are made, and upon which the success of the enterprise stands or falls.

A good illustration of this kind of family-operated business, in New Testament terms, is that reflected in the pericope of the calling of the first disciples:

And going along beside the sea of Galilee [Jesus] saw Simon and Andrew, Simon's brother, casting their nets in the sea, for they were fishermen. And Jesus said to them, "Come after me and I will make you fishers of men." And immediately leaving their nets they followed him. And proceeding a little farther he saw James, Zebedee's son, and his brother John, who were in their boat repairing their nets. And immediately he called them, and leaving their father, Zebedee, in the boat with the hired men they went away after him (Mark 1:16–20).

The fishing businesses of these two families had, in the

Graeco-Roman economy of Galilee, gotten beyond the
level of a cottage industry, but it was still by the combined
efforts of all in each family that they prospered. Simon
and Andrew were using the relatively simple casting nets
still used by fishermen in Galilee and along the shores of
the Mediterranean. This was a typical *mishpaḥah* or joint
family; for, a few verses farther on, reference is made to
Simon's mother-in-law from which we may infer that Simon and Andrew, though married, were still living in their
father's house, and that Simon's mother-in-law when feeling up to it still ran the house for the family (Mark 1:29–
31). Zebedee, the father in the other family, still operated
the fishing boat, giving orders not only to the hired men
but his sons as well. When this episode opened, all of them
—father, sons and hired hands—were engaged together in
the boat, repairing the dragnets in preparation for the next
day's foray.

With this kind of background we are now prepared to
return to the Ephesian passage with which we began. In
this passage the stewardship of the Church, here desig-
nated by the Pauline figure of "the body of Christ" (Ephesians 4:12), is set forth. The section opens with an exhortation addressed to Christians, for the author of the epistle
has addressed himself in the first instance to individuals—
"through the will of God to the saints [those sanctified by
baptism and adoption], who are also faithful [or trust-
worthy] in Christ Jesus" (Ephesians 1:1 c. p. 46 B°*Aleph*°
Mcion *et al.*). We shall see, however, that although this
exhortation is addressed to individuals, the author does not
and cannot conceive of them save within the *mishpaḥah*
of the Church which is God's family.

The author reminds his recipients that he himself is a
"prisoner of the Lord" (Ephesians 4:1). Paul's normal
mode of self-reference at the beginning of a letter is:
"Paul, a slave of Christ Jesus . . ." (Romans 1:1; Philip-

pians 1:1; compare Galatians 1:10), or "Paul, an apostle
of Christ Jesus, by the will of God . . ." (I Corinthians 1:1;
II Corinthians 1:1; Galatians 1:1; Romans 1:1). In Phile-
mon 1, he refers to himself as "a prisoner of Christ Jesus,"
and this same phrase occurs in Ephesians 3:1 and II Timothy 1:8 as well as here in Ephesians 4:1, but it means substantially the same thing as slave (*doulos*). This was an
apt description of the position held by the loyal member of
the joint family. The position is determined *dia thelēmatos
theou*, by God's will (I Corinthians 1:1; II Corinthians 1:1;
Ephesians 1:1; Colossians 1:1; II Timothy 1:1). The individual member of God's *mishpaḥah* has submitted himself to God's will; and presumably the author is addressing
himself to others who have at their baptisms said, "Abba,
Father" to God—"not my will but thine be done!"

The heart of the exhortation is, literally, that they shall
"walk worthily (*axiōs peripatēsai*) of their "calling,"
which is apparently a direct reference to the formal "calling" of the legal adoption procedure: namely, that God
the Father has called them "sons"! The verb used is the
one which provided the name for Aristotle's philosophical
school, the Peripatetics. It meant originally to pace back
and forth, which was Aristotle's manner when instructing
his students. However, a very common use of the verb in
the Hellenistic period meant "to live, conduct oneself, behave." It referred to one's general manner of living. Hence
the plea here is "to live worthily, to behave in a manner
worthy of one's calling in God's family."

There is a parallel exhortation in Philippians 1:27, in
which Paul uses the verb *politevein*, "Only conduct yourselves as citizens worthily of the gospel of Christ!" This is
to be understood, undoubtedly in connection with Philippians 3:20, where he says, "For our citizenship [*polite-
uma*] belongs [*huparchei*] in heaven, from whence we
long for a Savior, [our] Lord Jesus Christ." Paul's own

keen sense of appreciation of the rights, privileges, responsibilities, and dignity conferred by Roman citizenship, and the fact that he was addressing himself to persons who likewise appreciated these things, probably dictated his use of these terms. "To behave as a citizen" or "conduct oneself as a citizen" (*politevein*) probably carries a little more of the notion of responsible and dignified behavior than does the less colorful and more general term *peritatein*. For our particular purposes, both terms are quite legitimately the equivalent of *oikonomein*, "to be a trustworthy steward," in the house of the Father.

Serving as one of God's stewards requires humility (*tapeinophrosunē*), consideration (*prautēs*) of the other fellow, great patience (*makrothumia*), upholding one another in love (*anechomenoi allēlon en agapē*), and diligent guarding of the (family's) unity of Spirit in the bond of peace (*spoudazontes tēn henotēta tou pneumatos en tō sundesmō tēs eirēnēs*, Ephesians 4:1–3). It is obvious that if these are to be considered the characteristics of a trustworthy steward, what was said in Chapters 1 and 2 about the basically paternal, familial, and relational character of biblical stewardship is true. These are desirable traits whose main application is to intrafamily personal relationships.

Those things which are held in common by the family and which bind it together are next given in language that may well have served as a creed in the early Church. They also provide us with the basis for the *mishpaḥah* the solidarity which is the Church, the family of God. Even Gentile Christians "are no longer strangers and visitors, but . . . fellow-citizens of the saints and householders [*oikeioi*, members of the household] of God" (Ephesians 2:19). The various elements which bind this supra-ethnic *mishpaḥah* together are the following: A single body (the body of Christ), one Spirit (of which all have drunk, I

Corinthians 12:13), a single or common calling, one Lord, one faith, and one baptism (Ephesians 4:4–5). But crowning all these things held in common is this—note it well!—"One God and Father of [us] all, who is over all [in authority], permeates us all [with his life and purpose], and [lives] in us all, [the members of his household by his Spirit]" (Ephesians 4:6). The heavenly Father is the nucleus of the divine *mishpaḥah* as Abraham, being "father of the faithful," was the nucleus of the Hebrew *mishpaḥah*. It is God's *oikonomia*, his stewardship or economy, that binds all those who call him Father and who do his will into a single family. This is what makes them a family!

The Church—the Body of Christ

There is also significance in the order of elements at the beginning of this list. Neither Hebrew nor Greek required any particular word order for a sentence syntactically. It was common custom, therefore, for purposes of emphasis, for an author to use both the beginning and the end of a sentence, clause, phrase, or listing of things, for emphasis. In this list of unifying elements it is not accidental that the body is listed first. This is typically Pauline. The author has intended it for emphasis, for he was contending with the disruptive influences which were abroad in the Church of the late first century, and which had appeared in Thessalonica, Galatia, and Corinth at a very early date.

There were then, as there are now, those who, having been consciously or unconsciously influenced by one of the numerous forms of philosophical dualism, were insisting that a vague, undefinable "spiritual unity" was all that was required of Christians. This kind of thinking was characteristic of the gnosticism prevalent at Colossae, and of the docetism against which the Johannine writings were later directed. The author here, therefore, wishes to set things straight: "There is a single body!" and it has concrete reality! It is, of course, "the Church, which is the body of Christ" (Ephesians 1:23), the *mishpaḥah* of God! This is not some mystical esoteric, ectoplasmic wraith, but a real, live, physical, and visible body—as physical, visible, and identifiable as "the house of Israel" or "the house of Onesiphorus" (II Timothy 4:19).

It was impossible for anyone of orthodox Jewish background to conceive of an abstract "spiritual unity" apart from its manifestation in a body, and it was certainly not congenial to Paul's thought. Genesis 2 was regulative here. God took of the dust of the earth and formed the physical man, he then breathed into him his own Spirit, the breath of life, and at that point "man became a living soul *nephesh hayyāh*" (Genesis 2:7). It is inconceivable that body and spirit should exist separately if there is life. When they are separated, death ensues (Ecclesiastes 12:7). The *mishpaḥah*, therefore, is more than a group of people bound together by intangibles. It is a body, a house, a family that has a concrete physical manifestation in society. "There is a single body and one Spirit!" They have to go together.

Gifts of the Spirit

We come now to the places and functions assigned to individuals within the family of God. As in the family-operated businesses of Simon and Andrew, and of Zebedee and his sons, there were agreed-upon tasks for each to do. So it is in the household of God. This is suggested in verses 7 and 11. (We have omitted verses 8–10 since they are of a haggadic midrashic character and have little importance for the problem at hand.)

To each one of you grace was granted according to the measure of the gift of Christ . . . and he gave the apostles, and the prophets, and the evangelists, and the pastors and teachers (Ephesians 4:7, 11).

In order to set this within the Pauline context we must go back to the *locus classicus* in I Corinthians, Chapters 12 to 14, where Paul discusses spiritual gifts at greatest length and in considerable detail. He himself entitles this discourse *peri tōn pneumatikōn* (I Corinthians 12:1). The section which parallels Ephesians 4:7, 11 is found in I Corinthians 12:4–7.

So there are varieties of grace-gifts [*charismata*], but the same Spirit; and there are varieties of ministries [*diakoniai*] but the same Lord; and there are varieties of energizings [*energēmata*] but it is the same God who energizes them all in all saints [members of his family]. And the manifestation of the Spirit is given to each one for the common benefit [*pros to sumpheron*].

Then follows a list of *charismata:* "For to one a word of wisdom is given through the Spirit, to another a word of knowledge by the same Spirit." And so the list continues: faith, gifts of healings, energizings of miracles (*energē-mata dunameōn*), prophecy, distinguishing of spirits, kinds of tongues, and interpretation of tongues. Paul concludes the list: "And all of these [*charismata*] are energized by one and the same Spirit who by himself dispenses to each one just as he wishes" (I Corinthians 12:11).[6]

It is obvious from the great variety of gifts enumerated in lists of this kind—the gifts or fruits of the Spirit—that there was no carefully defined list (compare with Ephesians 4:11 the following: I Corinthians 12:8–10, 28; Galatians 5:22f; Romans 12:6–8; Philippians 4:8; Colossians 3:12–15). Actually these lists remind us very much of the lists of virtues, usually associated with lists of vices (see I Corinthians 6:9f; Galatians 5:19–21; Romans 1:29–31;

Colossians 3:5–8), which were so common in both pagan authors and Jewish literati such as Philo Judaeus. In the Pauline context whatever was a commendable virtue, useful in building up the body of Christ, was looked upon as a gift of the Spirit. They were the things that marked the newness of life, the signs of the presence of the Spirit, in the newly baptized convert.

It is obvious that Paul employs a number of general terms which are for him roughly synonymous in describing the particular gifts of the spirit of God to individuals. They are *pneumatika* (spiritual gifts), *charismata* (grace-gifts), *diakoniai* (ministries), *energēmata* (energizings), and *phanerōseis tou pneumatos* (manifestations of the Spirit). Each of these, of course, has its own peculiar nuance, however. *Pneumatika* suggests their divine source and inherent nature; *charismata* refers to their being reflections in the Christian of God's *charis* (grace); *diakoniai* infers the purpose and use for which they have been granted—not for self-indulgence but as ministries to be employed in behalf of others; *energēmata* indicates that they are infusions of particular abilities implanted in the individual by the Spirit; and *phanerōseis* implies that their Spirit-source is demonstrated by their presence in the Christian.

There are general similarities between Ephesians 4:7, 11 and I Corinthians 12:4–11, but there are also certain distinctions that should be noted. In I Corinthians Paul is discussing a great variety of gifts which in the early Church were recognized to have been granted to individuals by the coming of the Spirit upon them, normally following their baptism. Ephesians presents us rather with a list of commonly recognized functionaries in the Christian community. They should not be thought of as "church officers," as we use that term today, for the manner of their appointment or accession to the particular function which they exercised was probably in many cases simply by common acknowledgment. Paul himself, it will be recalled, was in the eyes of many "a self-appointed apostle" since he had not been in the original company of the Twelve; and he had to defend his apostleship on numerous occasions (for example, II Corinthians 1:21, 22; 2:17; 3:1–6; 5:11, 12; 10:8–18; 11:4–6; 11:12, 13; 12:11, 12; 13:3; Galatians 1:6–2:16; Philippians 1:15–18). He claims that he and Timothy "are not like the majority, peddlers [*kapēleuontes*] of God's word, but we speak out of sincerity, as from God, [being] in Christ" (II Corinthians 2:11). On the other hand he has little good to say for those other "apostles" who cast doubts on the authenticity of his own apostleship (II Corinthians 11:12, 13). He declares:

> For I am not at all inferior to these "superlative apostles" even if I am nothing. Indeed the signs [miracles] of the apostle were performed in your midst with all diligence: both signs, and wonders, and mighty-works (II Corinthians 12:11, 12).

There seem to have been great latitude, considerable difference in procedures, and no standardization of practices, all of which continued on into the subapostolic period. Probably this constitutes the very reason why Ephesians can substitute a list of primitive Christian functionaries for the particular gifts of the Spirit enumerated in I Corinthians. Both were pneumatic in their origins.

The second difference in the two passages lies in the fact that I Corinthians speaks of *charismata*, particular gifts of the Spirit being dispensed to individuals, whereas Ephesians is in terms of *charis*, or grace itself, being dispensed according to what Christ has determined, with the result that the Church is blessed with the various kinds of functionaries.

When Family Members Fulfill Their Functions

The point now is that God's household will function properly, and his economy or stewardship will achieve its end, as each member of the family enterprise takes his place and fulfills the function that may be expected of him, hence, Christ, the head of the body, in which God dwells by his Spirit, has provided that there should be apostles, prophets, evangelists, pastors, and teachers. "The manifestation of the Spirit is given to each for the common benefit" (I Corinthians 12:7). Or, as it is put in I Peter, "Whatever gift each of you may have received, use it in service to one another, like good stewards dispensing the grace of God in its varied forms" (I Peter 4:10).

We may say, then, that within the overarching economy of God, grace-gifts (*charismata*) are the particular gifts which the Holy Spirit in his stewardship dispenses to the saints. Once received by the saints they become their stewardship, "to be used in service to one another" in the Church and beyond it in the world. As those who employ their grace-gifts, they become God's stewards "dispensing the grace of God in its varied forms."

The Use of One's Talents

It is at this point that we should see the gospel roots of these ideas. There are a number of gospel logia bearing on the responsibility of the individual to make use of what God has given him; but the two best-known parables on this theme are, of course, those of the talents (Matthew 25:14–28) and of the pounds (Luke 19:12–24). They differ in some points and, whether these differences are original and there were actually two distinct parables coming down in the oral tradition, or the differences arose in the course of oral transmission—which seems on the whole more plausible—their main purport is the same. In God's economy his servants, the members of his household, are expected to use what has been granted them by the head of the household, for the best interests of the household. They have been entrusted the pounds or the talents, not only for safekeeping but for investment and increase. In both cases the servant who returned his master's funds intact is called, "Thou wicked servant!"

Our English word "talent" is derived from the Greek *talanton* from which, in turn, the Latin *talentum* was derived. Both were sizable ingots of metal (gold, silver, or copper) used for exchange. But very early in Christian interpretation, as Professor C. H. Dodd has insisted, "the parable of the money in trust was used to illustrate the maxim that a man who possesses spiritual capacity will enlarge that capacity by experience, while a man who has none will decline into a worse condition as time goes on." [7] Dodd believes that this was interpreted in the early Church, prior to the production of the Gospel According to Matthew, as a commentary on the logion of Jesus in Mark 4:25: "For him who has, it shall be given him; and him who has not, even what he has shall be taken away." [8] As a matter of fact, it is not difficult to see Mark's reason for Jesus' habit of resorting to parables as a didactic method interpreted in this way also: "To you has been granted the secret [*mustērion*] of the kingdom of God; but to those outside all things take place in parables so that 'Seeing they may see and not perceive, and hearing they may hear and not understand, lest they should repent and it be forgiven them'" (Mark 4:11, 12).

It was only another brief step for the Church to take the term "talent" and apply it to the gifts of the Spirit bestowed upon the Christian at or following his baptism. And a final step was taken when it became possible in the Christian West to define talent as Webster defines it: "The abilities, powers, and gifts bestowed upon a man; natural endowments;—thought of as a divine trust."

There is, of course, a physical parallel to this intellectual and spiritual assertion which undoubtedly contributed to its popularity and commended it to reason (Mark 4:25// Matthew 13:12// Luke 8:18; Matthew 25:29// Luke 19: 26). Atrophy is known to take place when muscles and other parts of the human system go unused for long periods of time. They may even become completely useless, whereas muscles that are used regularly and vigorously become stronger. The Jew would have argued by a *qal we-hōmĕr* argument that if this be true in the physical realm, how much more true it would be in the intellectual and spiritual realms.

Christ's gifts to the Church of apostles, prophets, evangelists, pastors, and teachers were for two quite specific purposes: (1) "for the preparation of the saints for the work of service or ministry [*diakonia*]"; and (2) "for the building up of the body of Christ . . . until . . . all arrive . . . at mature manhood" (Ephesians 4:12, 13). They were in order that God's family, the *mishpaḥah,* might function perfectly, each member taking his full share of the task according to his gifts. These five categories of functionaries are equally charged with responsibility for the preparation of the saints for their work of ministry, that is, to give them individually all possible assistance in the development and exercise of their gifts; and also for the building up of the body collectively as a *mishpaḥah* or family.

As in I Corinthians 13, Ephesians 4:15 urges Christians to be truthful, or to behave with integrity (*alētheuontes*), in love. "Love . . . is the bond of perfectness" (Colossians 3:14), which is required "to knit [the family] together [*sum bibasthentes en agapē,* Colossians 2:2; compare *sum bibazomenon,* Ephesians 4:16]." The members of the family are expected to "uphold one another in love" (Ephesians 4:2). And when all are responsibly bearing their share, this "produces the growth of the body by the measure of each individual part" (Ephesians 4:16). The growth of the body here is not the maturing of each individual member, but the growth of the entire corporate body—the Church, the family of God.

The stewardship of the functionaries, therefore, is to assist the saints to Christian maturity; and the stewardship of the saints is to develop their talents, their *charismata,* to the fullest degree, and to contribute them for the building up of the Church by using them "in service to one another, like good stewards dispensing the grace of God" (I Peter 4:10).

Motivation for Giving

What now may be said about motivation for giving on the basis of the collective stewardship of the Church? Obviously, first of all, one may not make a unilateral decision about a gift of self, time, talents, property, or funds; for a Christian does not act in isolation, but rather as a son and heir in the household of his heavenly Father. He should be motivated because of his loyalty to the Father to whom with all in the house he has acknowledged his subjection, but he should also be motivated by his loyalty to the rest of the family whose corporate joys and labors he shares.

Again he should be motivated by the knowledge of what the family enterprise embraces—a plan or stewardship for the fullness of the times, to bring all things to completion in Christ—that the entire universe (*ho kosmos*) may be reconciled to God. He should be motivated by the love and grace of God that have flooded his life in the fellowship of God's family. He should be motivated, too, by the conscious and painful knowledge that these blessings he shares in the commonwealth (*politeia*) of God and the covenants of promise are still unknown to those who are separated from Christ and who, being without God, have no hope in the world (Ephesians 2:12). It is the family's purpose, first, to reach all such with the good news that "God was in Christ reconciling the world to himself" and that he therefore "no longer holds men's misdeeds against them"; and, second, to realize the inclusion of all men within the *mishpaḥah* of God, in the unity of faith and of the revelation of the son of God, and to bring them the full maturity which Christ exhibited in his own life and makes available to all members of the family.

NOTES FOR CHAPTER 3

1. *Lexicon in Veteris Testamenti Libros,* Ludwig Koehler and Walter Baumgartner (Grand Rapids, Mich.: Wm. B. Eerdmans Publishing Co.).
2. *From the Stone Age to Christianity* (Baltimore: Johns Hopkins Press, 1940), pp. 186ff. Used by permission.
3. (London: Oxford University Press, 1926, 1946), Vol. I-II, p. 48. By permission of Oxford University Press, Inc., New York.
4. *Ibid.,* Vol. I-II, p. 50.
5. *Hebrew Man* (London: Student Christian Movement Press, 1956), p. 89. Used by permission.
6. Taking *idia* adverbially, C. W. Bauer, *Lexicon: idios, ia, on,* 4 and not in apposition to *ekastō.*
7. *The Parables of the Kingdom* (New York: Charles Scribner's Sons, 1936), p. 149.
8. *Ibid.,* pp. 148, 152.

QUESTIONS FOR DISCUSSION

1. Does God have a plan for each congregation?
2. Does God have a plan for each denomination?

4

Good Stewards
of God's Grace

"WHATEVER gift each of you may have received, use it in service to one another, like good stewards dispensing the grace of God in its varied forms." (NEB, I Peter 4:10.)

First Peter was written to Christians living in the Roman provinces of Asia Minor at a time when their confession of Christ's name brought with it severe persecution. Pliny the Younger (circa A.D. 62–114), who was a Roman governor in Asia in the early second century, wrote his Emperor, Trajan, that "this contagious superstition [he was referring to Christianity] . . . has spread through the villages and rural districts," and that those who are denounced to him as Christians he ordered to be executed unless "they . . . worshipped [Trajan's] statue and the images of the gods and cursed Christ." In some such circumstances this Epistle was written.

"The end of all things is upon us," the Epistle says, "so you must lead an ordered and sober life, given to prayer" (4:7). "The time has come for judgment to begin; it is beginning with God's own household" (4:17).

My dear friends, do not be bewildered by the fiery ordeal that is upon you, as though it were something extraordinary. It gives you a share in Christ's sufferings, and that is cause for joy and when his glory is revealed, your joy will be triumphant. If Christ's name is flung in your teeth as an insult, count yourselves happy, because then that glorious Spirit, which is the Spirit of God, is resting upon you (I Peter 4:12–14).

Have no fear of them: do not be perturbed, but hold the Lord Christ in reverence in your hearts. Be always ready with your defense whenever you are called to account for the hope that is in you, but make that defense with modesty and respect. Keep your conscience clear so that when you are abased, those who malign your Christian conduct may be put to shame. It is better to suffer for well-doing, if such should be the will of God, than for doing wrong (I Peter 3:14–17).

Under such circumstances Christians are always driven back to essentials—to those fundamental elements without which Christian faith is unidentifiable as such. It is not surprising, therefore, that we discover in I Peter one of the finest definitions of Christian stewardship to be found anywhere in the New Testament. The New English Bible renders it this way:

Whatever gift each of you may have received, use it in service to one another, like good stewards dispensing the grace of God in its varied forms (4:10).

Grace-Gifts of the Spirit

The word translated "gift" in this verse is *charisma*, the word used in the Pauline letters for the grace-gifts of the Spirit bestowed upon those who are baptized into the body of Christ. There can be no doubt that I Peter builds upon a Pauline foundation. The classical Pauline treatment of these grace-gifts is in I Corinthians, chapters 12 to 14, where the endowments of the Spirit are discussed at considerable length. Man is saved by grace (*charis*) through faith (*pistis*). In one sense we can say that when man's faith responds to God's grace he is saved; but in another sense even man's faith is God's gift: "This is not your own doing, it is the gift of God" (Ephesians 2:8).

The Spirit is the mediator or dispenser of God's grace to believers, initially through their baptism into Christ through which all have been made to drink of the same Spirit. The particular manifestations of the grace (*charis*) of God to the individual are variously called grace-gifts (*charismata*), spiritual gifts (*pneumatikoi*), ministries (*diakoniai*), energizings (*energēmata*), and manifestations of the Spirit (*phanerōseis tou pneumatos*).

Paul says, "To each one is granted the manifestation of the Spirit for the common good." The Spirit of God, therefore, is the primary agent through whom these grace-gifts are bestowed upon an individual; and the gifts are granted "for the common good." In the same passage Paul speaks of a wide variety of grace-gifts: wisdom, knowledge, faith, healing, miracles, prophecy. In Romans 12 he gives a somewhat different list: prophecy, ministry, teaching, exhortation, charity, mercy, love. In I Corinthians 13 we learn that the supreme grace-gift, which all should seek, is love. I Peter also intimates that all grace-gifts are "for the common good": "Whatever gift each of you may have received, use it in service to one another." The phrase is participial in construction—literally, "ministering (*diako-nountes*) it to one another." This is the same verb, *diako-nein*, which is used in Matthew 20:28, "For the Son of man came not to be ministered to, but to minister, and to give his life as a ransom for many." Christ himself has set the example. God's grace is given, not for the sole enjoyment of the recipient, but in trust, to be used for, and passed on to, others. There is a stewardship involved! This is why the verse in I Peter goes on to add, "like good stewards [*kaloi oikonomoi*] dispensing the grace of God in its varied forms."

The Christian—a Channel of God's Grace to Others

Though the Spirit of God is the primary agent in dispensing God's grace, this does not rule out God's use of Christians as secondary agents. In the introduction to the Roman letter Paul writes, "I long to see you, in order that I may impart [*hina metadō*] to you some spiritual grace-gift [*ti charisma pneumatikon*] that you may be strengthened, that is to say, that we may be mutually encouraged, each by the faith of the other, both yours and mine" (Romans 1:11, 12). Thus it is that in the Christian community individuals become channels—the secondary or intermediate agents—of God's grace to others. But this is true not only within the Christian community, but outside it in the world at large. The gospel is the good news "that God was in Christ reconciling the world to himself, no longer holding men's misdeeds against them" (II Corinthians 5:19). The gospel is "God's power for salvation to everyone who has faith." When God's servants bear witness to the gospel, whether by word or in Christlike service, to their fellow men they are the channels of God's grace. Thus they recognize and exercise their stewardship, "dispensing the grace of God in its varied forms," as I Peter puts it.

One does not have to be an apostle, a prophet, a presbyter, or a deacon to share in this stewardship. It belongs to all Christians. Professor Beare points out, "The *charismata* are the various endowments which God imparts to all the members of the community, not to the leaders alone, natural aptitudes are heightened, and new powers are awakened by His presence within us, that all may be enabled to serve the community in some measure." [1] The basic purpose in granting the various grace-gifts to individuals is that they may be employed in building up the Church (*tēn ekklesian oikodomein*, I Corinthians 14:4, 12, 19, 26).

Inner and Outer Dimensions of the Church

Building up the Church always has in Paul's understanding a twofold dimension. There is both an inner and an outer dimension. The first may be described as nurture and the second as mission. The first is directed inwardly toward the Church, and the second is directed outwardly to the world. Moreover, the first is not an end in itself, but the means to the end of the second. Nurture is in order to mission.

Nurture is what happens in this reciprocal action that takes place within the Christian community when each member exercises his stewardship of God's grace in its varied forms. Each contributes the exercise of the gifts granted him by the Spirit for the common good, and in turn each finds himself strengthened and encouraged by the faith of others. This is what takes place in the daily fellowship (*koinonia*) in common worship (*leitourgia*) and in the mutual service (*diakonia*) of one another within the community. All this is developed in theory in I Corinthians 12 in Paul's figure of the body with its many members, and it is developed pragmatically in I Corinthians 14, particularly in terms of the common worship of the Church.

But, as we have said, nurture is not an end in itself. It is not only for the gratification of the desires and needs of the members of the community. Rather, it is the major means to the major end of the Church, which is its mission to the world in behalf of Christ. Christians are entrusted with the message of reconciliation, and have been granted a ministry of reconciliation. They are Christ's ambassadors, through whom God makes his appeal to men. The Church is built up in the sense of self-nurturing only that it may understand and be obedient to the will of God, that it may carry out the purposes of God in and for the world, that the world may be fully reconciled to God and Christ.

It is the eschatological dimension of the mission, which may also be described as its cosmic dimension, that makes it and keeps it mission (*apostellein*), a sending away, or a sending out. Any concept of mission that is devoid of this eschatological-cosmic dimension, or that is content with anything less, is an emasculated concept. It is not, and cannot be, mission in its fundamental New Testament sense. The Johannine Christ says, "As the Father has sent me [*apostellein*] even so I send you."

Everything in the Church's life must be oriented around this sense of outwardly directed mission. All that the Church does may be justified only by the contributions it makes to that mission. This is why Paul never loses sight of his having been appointed a missionary to the Gentile nations. The world is to be reconciled to God in Jesus Christ, and the ministry and message of that reconciliation have been committed to the Church. The gospel is good news for all men. The gospel is "God's power for salvation to every one who exercises faith." To each Christian the *charismata* have been granted for the common good, for the building up of the body of Christ, inwardly through its nurture, but ultimately and outwardly through its mission, until it embraces all men. Even though Paul gave up, temporarily, his hope for the immediate salvation of his own nation, he foresaw the time when they all would be saved after the fullness of the Gentile harvest (Romans 11:25).

Biblical stewardship is then always related to purpose and to goals. It can never be divorced from them. It cannot be abstracted as a pious discipline or an ethical principle. It is rather the basic response of man to the grace of God. Other frequently used terms for this response are worship (*leitourgia*) and service (*diakonia*).

Worship, Service, and Stewardship

In the author's own Church, the vows of membership, which do not vary greatly from those of other communions, begin with a declaration of one's personal faith in Jesus Christ as Lord and Savior. The second vow is a promise "to make diligent use of the means of grace," but this in turn is then spelled out more fully: "to share faithfully in the worship [*leitourgia*] and service [*diakonia*] of the Church," and "to give of [one's] substance [*oikonomia*] as the Lord may prosper [one]." "Diligent use of the means of grace" is thus understood as responsible participation in the worship, service, and support of the Church. By such participation one shares actively in the life of Christ's body, and is sustained as a veritable member of that body. To use the Johannine figure, this is the way the branches abide in the vine, who is Jesus Christ. "The branch cannot bear fruit of itself, except it abide in the vine; so neither can ye, except ye abide in me" (John 15:4). We draw our life from the body, and in turn we contribute our life, our strength, to the body. That is to say, we use the life we draw from the body in behalf of the body itself, and for the reconciling and redemptive purposes for which the body exists.

Worship, service, and stewardship are thus ways God has chosen by which our lives are merged creatively with his life. They are means by which his grace flows into our lives. But they are much more than that. They are also the means by which his grace flows through our lives into the lives of others. When we worship together as the gathered people of God, a psychic community is established whereby, as Paul put it, each of us is strengthened by the faith of the other.

When we render a service in Christ's name, God's grace flows through us into the life of someone else, and in the process we find our own lives blessed and enriched. The widow's unfailing cruse of oil is a parable of this spiritual truth. The more it is used, the more there is to be used. And again, when we render a responsible steward-ship for Christ's sake, whether it be in meeting the mate-rial or the spiritual needs of our fellow men, our exercise of that stewardship becomes a channel of God's grace to others and, in the process, to ourselves as well. Here we discover the truth of the Lord's word, "It is more blessed to give than to receive." Worship, service, and stewardship are then means of grace both to others and to ourselves.

Worship, service, and stewardship are all terms ex-pressive of man's response to God's grace, but each em-phasizes a different aspect of that response. Worship is man's spontaneous adoration of God for the gift of his grace. Service is man's action in behalf of God and in be-half of his fellow men which is called forth in response to God's act in Christ on man's behalf. Stewardship is man's acknowledgment that all he has, has come from God, and that he therefore owes all he has to God. It is his recogni-tion that he is entrusted with these gifts as God's steward.

These three terms, moreover, may be interpreted in such ways that any one of them can become the generic or organizing principle, of which the other two in each case are functions or expressions. For instance, worship may be considered the radical term, so that service and steward-ship are conceived as forms of worship. *Laborare orare est!* "To work is to pray." "Contributing to the needs of the saints," with its origins in Jewish almsgiving, is understood by Paul to be an act of worship (I Corinthians 16:1-2, Romans 12:13). Or we may make service the basic term, with worship and stewardship seen as forms of service, which indeed they are. Or, again, stewardship may be made the decisive concept, with worship and service con-sidered as functions of stewardship.

When stewardship is understood in its broadest sense, it cannot be limited to the responsible management of one's material possessions—to the giving "of [our] substance as the Lord may prosper [us]." It involves all that man is, really and potentially, as well as all that he possesses. It includes the responsible management and use of his knowledge, training, and experience, of his abilities and skills, and of his time and energy. It is a stewardship of the whole person as well as of all the material things under his supervisory control. Nothing less can suffice. This is what God demands and expects.

This is the stewardship of which I Peter speaks. "The *charismata* are the concrete manifestations of the *charis* [grace] that has been bestowed." [2] They represent an infinite variety and richness. The examples which follow our text refer specifically to *charismatic* or prophetic preaching (*lalein*) and to *charismatic* service (*diakonein*), the latter "embracing all kinds of Christian work except preaching" [3] namely, service in its personal active doing on behalf of others.

Are you a speaker? [Then] speak as if you uttered oracles of God. Do you give service? [Then] give it as in the strength which God supplies. [4]

Speaking and serving are thus general categories that cover all the kinds of *charismatic* grace-gifts with which Christians are endowed.

The Use of Possessions—a Test of Faith

How does it happen that we so often limit stewardship to the narrower concept of the stewardship of material possessions, or, even more narrowly, of money alone? The answer is really not difficult to come by. Stewardship of possessions has, from man's most primitive religious expressions, been a symbol of his broader, more comprehensive stewardship. Among the ancient Hebrews, for instance, the corn and oil offerings, the first-fruit cereal offerings, the wine libations, the first-born lamb were all interpreted as symbolic of the belief that the entire crop, the whole grain harvest, the annual yield of olive oil and wine, and all one's flocks and herds were God's gift to man. By virtue of this belief man was called upon to husband all these gifts with the utmost care. Each of these offerings of portions of man's substance amounted to a recognition that man owed all he had to the God who had given him of his bounty.

But the stewardship of substance is also more than a symbol of man's total stewardship. It is, in fact, a proof, a demonstration, a verification of the acknowledgment of such total stewardship. It thus becomes a test of the sincerity of man's faith in God; for, as Jesus pointed out to his contemporaries, "Where your treasure is, there will your heart be also." This simple observation was based upon an accurate understanding of human nature.

If a man is truly committed to the doing of God's will, this will demonstrate itself in his stewardship. The kingdom of heaven or the kingdom of God—the two terms are interchangeable—which simply means "acknowledgment of God's sovereignty," is like "hidden treasure" or a "pearl of great price." It is worth the liquidation of all one's assets to gain possession of that sovereignty, to yield fully to the stewardship which that sovereignty demands.

Our text from I Peter is addressed to those who have acknowledged God's sovereignty. They have been sanctified, that is, "set apart" or "consecrated" by the Spirit for obedience to Jesus Christ (I Peter 1:2). It is to such persons that the words of our text are addressed:

Whatever grace-gift you may have received, use it in service to one another, like good stewards dispensing the grace of God in its varied forms.

Notes for Chapter 4

1. Francis Wright Beare, ed., *The First Epistle of Peter* (Oxford: Blackwell; and New York: The Macmillan Company, 1947), p. 159f.
2. Beare, *op. cit.*, p. 161.
3. *Ibid.*
4. Beare's translation of I Peter 4:11.

Questions for Discussion

1. If grace is always a gift of God, how can Christians work to receive it?
2. Is it possible to give God any gift directly, or do all gifts to God reach him through service to others? What is the relationship of "worship" and "service"?

Part II

CORPORATE
STEWARDSHIP

by Joseph C. McLelland

**Professor of Philosophy of Religion,
McGill University, Montreal, Canada**

5

The Congregation

A TEACHING device to end with definitions is generally better than one to begin with them, so that the discussion of the subject can prepare for precise meaning. However, in the present case we need to begin with certain preliminary definitions, to indicate our "terms of reference," and so to outline the themes we shall treat. There are two terms to be defined at the outset: "corporate" and "benevolence."

By "corporate stewardship" we shall mean those structures which are both accountable for their own stewardship, and also responsible for the provision of an environment that will encourage proper stewardship in the members. Our appointed task is to examine three such structures: the congregation, the denomination, and the nation. We shall view all these as open to analysis in terms of the nature of power structures or human institutions, familiar to us through the work of sociologists.[1] We shall be prepared to treat the Church as—among other things— a human institution, and the state as—among other things —a power ordained by God. So we make no apology for drawing on sociological insights when examining the Church, or theological in regard to the state. Ours is a society in which power structures have changed and grown

so that Christian vocation and stewardship are almost entirely irrelevant, like an old-fashioned maiden aunt de-
posited at a college beach party and trying to express her
idea of morality.

We professional clergymen especially have become a
sort of curio, an interesting specimen of outdated behavior
patterns, still encouraged within the Church but not relevant to real life in the world. Now we mean in all sincerity that even our laymen share this view, that they too
find what we have to say about stewardship applicable
only within the congregational and denominational life—
a bit of domestic housekeeping. They do not find it helpful
outside the Church, in the world where they earn the
money we take for granted in stewardship.

Second, this conference concerns "benevolence promotion." We shall take this to mean not only the general care
program of traditional stewardship, but also the special
bias of Christian giving toward the needy, the dispos-
sessed, the outcast. This will provide a test against which
to measure both congregation and denomination: is their
stewardship loaded in this direction, or is it directed chiefly
toward themselves, toward their institutional preservation?
And it may serve as a test of the nation too, as we shall see.

The Congregational "We"

What is a congregation? It is a group, a "body" of people
doing certain things together. We speak of "corporate
worship" when we describe the group's gathering on Sunday morning. The liturgical renewal which is sweeping
through all churches has helped us to see that this means
more than several people doing their private devotions at
the same time and place! That has always been a primary
error in our liturgy—Roman as well as Protestant. It was
not truly *corporate* worship, but only an appearance of

group activity. The church worship simply offered a time and place for various people to do similar acts. There was (and is, where this error continues) no genuine offering of *common* prayers, no hearing the Word of God as a congregation, no looking upon the Eucharist as the body of Christ. Now I introduce this liturgical phenomenon here to suggest that this provides a striking parallel to what we do in our stewardship. Too often we are not united in our stewardship, but operate only as a variety of people doing certain things—using time, talent, and treasure—in similar ways. Because we all belong to the same congregation, we can speak of a stewardship "program" in which we participate. But it is not necessarily *corporate* stewardship unless we act together as a cohesive unit toward the goal of the program.

You will see that corporate stewardship implies a certain view of the Church, an ecclesiology. It assumes that the congregation possesses a unity which derives not only from the common interests and commitments of its members, but also from the peculiar relationship of this group to its Head. Theologians used to speak of this as a "real and substantial" union of the believers with Christ—men like John Calvin, for example, who had learned about the unity of the Church from ancient Fathers such as Cyprian and Augustine. Augustine has a most interesting (if difficult!) doctrine of unions: Father, Son, and Holy Spirit are consubstantial within the Trinity; the divine and the human are hypostatically one in Jesus Christ; Christians are really and substantially one with Christ and with one another. So the unifying power at work in the Church constitutes the congregation, a group which by definition must function as a corporate entity or else it is not true to its nature and calling. This is the congregational "we," the speaking with one voice which is more than an editorial device or a human convention. The pronouncements of the Pope are always constructed in the plural, since he is considered to be the visible symbol of this unified humanity, the Church. Now I suggest that this typically Western idea is not so helpful—particularly in talking of stewardship—as the ecclesiology of the Eastern Church.

The difference in ecclesiology between West and East may be stated somewhat as follows. In the West, the Church has been understood primarily as *universal:* "according to the whole" (*kat' holos*). Therefore, local churches are considered as parts of the whole, or as branches, or as administrative provinces. Inevitably we in the West tend to think of the "real" Church as the hierarchy, the professionals, the headquarters staff. But in the East, it is the local church, the congregation as worshiping community, which is the real church—the Church present in all its wholeness. The larger groupings do not make the Church present in larger part, but constitute rather a different sort of reality: the family of churches, the unity of this variety. This Eastern view, by the way, is becoming more important in the Church of Rome, where the idea that the bishop is the local representative of the Pope is being challenged by the idea that the bishop is the representative of the local church, identifiable as that which "in some manner presents the visible Church constituted throughout the world." [2]

It is in this latter sense that we are right to begin with the congregation; for in the local Christian community, in the worshiping group gathered on the Lord's Day, we have the normative "church." Regardless of its polity, the Church is always "congregational" in this meaning of the concrete, localized gathering. Therefore, corporate stewardship refers primarily to what this group does with its material—its time, talent, and treasure. If its congregational "we" is spoken through these means, then there is genuine stewardship. But if it fails to express its nature as Christ's people in this place through stewardship, but remains content with general directives or exhortation, then it has failed to *be* the Church.

Stewardship is no optional alternative for the congregation; it is the very stuff of its life together. It embodies or "incorporates" the community's faith; apart from genuine stewardship there is only a spirituality which pretends to be the result of the Holy Spirit, but is not. How do we know what sort of spirituality is appropriate to the Holy Spirit? Because the Spirit is Christ's Spirit, who effects a new creation in the likeness of Christ, who creates a new humanity participating in the continuing presence and power of the King and Head of the Church. The Holy Spirit, that is to say, is never a formless operator, but is known by his effects, his fruits, the form of new humanity. He is the Spirit who proceeds from the mutual love of the Father and the Son, so that he is by definition the Spirit of relationship, unity, reconciliation, integration. The community created by the Spirit can have only one kind of stewardship: corporate stewardship.

The Group for Other Groups

We said in beginning that sociology would be accepted as a valid discipline for viewing the Church, at least from one realistic angle. The Church is new humanity, but this is still human—a group or institution or organization that operates in large part in response to similar behavior patterns observable in all group life. One of the first Christians to recognize this was Dietrich Bonhoeffer, whose early writing *Sanctorum Communio* sought to benefit from a sociological analysis of the Christian community while developing a most helpful ecclesiology.[3] For example, Bonhoeffer's understanding of the church may be summed up in his phrase, "Christ existing as community." The church is a form of Christ's own existence, part of the mystery of the divine-human relationship established by and in our Lord himself. Although it is similar to the familiar description, "extension of the incarnation," it is free from the temptation to consider it as something on its own, established by a law of its own being, gifted and graced apart from the continuing presence of Christ himself. So it is that both exist together, the sociological and the christological analyses of the congregation. For the Church is both *koinonia* and "institution," inseparably together, each informing the other.[4]

In recent years the analysis of the Church has progressed to the point where various alternatives or solutions are being offered. One of the most influential debates is that between the Peter Berger school and the Winter-Marty line. The former sees little hope of making the traditional church structure fit for service in the new world already upon us; the latter thinks there can be genuine reformation and renewal by which the Church can meet the situation. The debate revolves about the significance of urbanization. "Metropolis" is the new creation which society has developed, but which the Church cannot serve in its present form because the pattern of parochial and congregational life was not shaped by the needs of industrialized, urbanized modern man. The Church is victim of class division, patriotic demands, institutional drag, and continuing clericalism. This summary is not meant to be a caricature, but to suggest the general lines of debate and the serious challenge which the analysts bring. If any of you have tried to introduce the analysis to suburbia, you will know how difficult it is to get a hearing; and this too is a symptom of the dis-ease of the congregation today.

A *Typical Congregation*

What is a typical congregation? Certainly the sociologists operate with "idealized types," yet so do we all. Theologians tend to think of the Church as made up of students who need to be taught. Stewardship officials think of the Church as a potential, a resource, waiting to be organized properly through the techniques of benevolence promotion. Sociologists point out that urbanization is probably the greatest fact to be faced in thinking of the modern congregation: even the "rural" area is more like its sister in the metropolis than its counterpart in former generations. It is as if we all inhabit a city, made up of a series of concentric circles. At the center is the "inner city," consisting of business district and adjacent slum. We all are affected by the decisions made downtown, and many of us commute into that environment from suburban residences. The Church exists in the inner city either as a building to which stalwart old folk still make their long way each Sunday, or as an experimental inner city mission beloved by seminarians and professors of social ethics. Most people, however, think of the typical member of the Church in suburban developments as the organization man, wearing his gray flannel suit, taking the 5:15 home to Fertile Crescent in Crestwood Heights, where he has a couple of cocktails with his neighbor's wife before attacking the crabgrass. Behind the caricature, make no mistake about it, lurks a sinister distortion of what a congregation really is.

The tragedy of suburbia is that its churches accept its cultural pattern and minister only to the community at hand. Once upon a time this would have been good, when the idea of the "parish" was realistic and the community was a varied whole reflecting the larger society. But in suburbia we have an artificial, partial community, a residential and educational and recreational community.

These are personal values and goals rather than public responsibilities and decisions, so that the gulf between the downtown inner city and the suburb is widened by typical suburban activities. If the churches in suburbia were truly the prophetic voice, the seminary for rebels, the social conscience, then the divorce would not be so decisive. But usually our suburban congregations are ingrown, concerned only with the "private sphere" of faith, or, as it has been put, "the residential community organized for local religion." Now it is not that suburbia is unusual: on the contrary, the reason why it is the subject of so much analysis is that it has become the typical church, the hope of church renewal, and the key to "church extension" programs currently sweeping our denominations. It is the new representative congregation; therefore it must accept its responsibility as the test case.

Mission to Other Groups

The sociological analysis is good and necessary, because the Church is truly human, one group among others. Yet it is the miracle and mystery of grace that God uses things truly human; he is present in and through this group in particular. Bonhoeffer's phrase was "Christ existing as community." Since he described Christ as "the man for others" could we not therefore describe the Church as "the group for other groups"? To view the congregation christologically means to accept all that sociology has to say and then to reconstruct this group along lines dictated by Christ's own form of existence. As he lived "for" others, so must the congregation live for its community, as the group which is a sign of genuine community. In the disintegration of modern life together, it provides an "integration center" (what a loaded word for this continent!). In the midst of competition from all sorts of groups—service clubs, PTA, Little League Coaches, Inc.–it issues a calm invitation to consider Christ's calling. In a word, it has a *mission* to all other groups; that is what corporate stewardship means. If it thinks only of the individuals who attend, or the private sphere of faith, then it fails to recognize the distinctive contribution it has to make to *community*, to group dynamics. It has two chief means of being such a sign, and together they constitute its stewardship.

L + D = O

The little equation L + D = O appears on some of the stewardship literature of this author's own denomination, and sums up the three terms common in the New Testament description of congregational life: worship (*leitourgia*), service (*diakonia*), and stewardship (*oikonomia*). The terms are almost interchangeable; but, as the equation suggests, corporate stewardship involves the two poles of worship and service, which focus Christian responsibility in a motion toward God and toward man. Dr. T. M. Taylor has illustrated their relationship in Chapter 1 of this book, a commentary on I Peter 4:10 (NEB): "Whatever gift each of you may have received, use it in service to one another, like good stewards dispensing the grace of God in its varied forms." It is at this point that I should like to see our stewardship literature take a bold step forward, to insist that the decisive term must be *service*. We know that all God's commandments were summed up in two: love God and the neighbor (Mark 12:28). But Jesus himself made clear that you love God *by* loving the neighbor (Matthew 25:31ff), and Paul stated: "The whole law is fulfilled in one word, 'You shall love your neighbor as yourself'" (Galatians 5:14, RSV). It was a favorite theme of Luther and Calvin that we love and honor and serve God indirectly, through the neighbor, when we love and honor and serve our fellow men. Commenting on the incarnation, Luther said: "For this was the reason why he put off the form of God and took on the form of a servant, that he might draw down our love for him and fasten it on our neighbor."

The congregation at worship, in view of this latter point, is the congregation offering God its obedience to his will that it serve its community. The significance of Sunday worship ("divine service") for stewardship is not simply that it provides an opportunity to collect the offering envelopes! Rather, here is the group gathered because of the "common Spirit" which constitutes it the steward of God's mysteries. Is it not high time that we recovered this primary orientation of stewardship, the fact that we are stewards of the Word and Sacraments, and *therefore* stewards of time, talent, and treasure? It is not just that everything we have is God's gift; but that some things (the Word of God in all his forms) are never ours to possess, but only to transmit. When "all sorts and conditions of men" gather not because of common interests or common residence or common tradition, but because despite their variety God has enlightened them with joy in his Word— then you have the presence of the group for all others. To celebrate God's Word is to join worship with service, to raise up a sign that this is not a "religious" group but a group conformed to the strange new form of Christ, existing as community. Just as Jesus himself once offered God a sacrificial service of his fellow men, outside the religious establishment, so this group must learn that it is called to do likewise. The idea of going "beyond religion" is familiar enough by this time; but have we seen its meaning for congregations?

It is the gospel itself which is the "inexpressible gift" handed down to us for stewardship (see I Corinthians 15:3, "I delivered . . . what I received . . . that Christ died

for our sins . . .").[5] As the worshiping congregation celebrates the gospel each Lord's Day, it fulfills the decisive
part of its stewardship, and establishes the proper foundation for its life of service. For instance, here is that congregational context for "vocational guidance" so necessary
for stewardship, as Christians are nurtured to understand
their own "gifts of grace" (*charismata*) by which Christ
intends that the congregation should be ordered. One's
natural "talents" are surely to be evaluated in this context
also, so that all life is present in worship, searched out by
God's Word in sermon, offered to God in sacrament. Indeed, the whole point about letting things be done "de-
cently and in order" (I Corinthians 14:40) was to curb the
esoteric and ingrown nature of speaking in tongues, so that
congregational worship would constitute an intelligible
sign to the world.

"House"

The congregation is the house that God built. It is *oikos*
because it is corporate, grouped, like a family. This household of God should be given to hospitality, for brotherly
love means the entertaining of strangers. It also means
something notably lacking from much stewardship literature, the sharing of *suffering*. I Peter 4, a remarkable
passage for stewardship, talks equally about hospitality,
witness, service, and sharing in Christ's sufferings. The
last is nothing strange (verse 12) but part of Christian
involvement in Christ—existing as community. It is God's
will indeed, for judgment begins at God's house. This
group lives for others, and suffers for them. It is an open
society, hospitable to every kind of person, accepting them
in Christ. It is as reckless as Christ was in befriending the
outcast, as prodigal as he was in bestowing its love.

The congregational *leitourgia* must combine with *dia-*

konia if genuine stewardship is to be carried on. This is why stewardship cannot be adulterated into a mere challenging of members to support the local institution, to care for the plant as an end in itself. It is mission that provides the test: a group geared for mission to the community—local and larger—can justify spending money on itself insofar as this aids in preparation for mission. The "sanctuary" is not an absolute end in itself, as if our task were to get the whole community inside. That was the dream of Christendom long ago, and the old parish mentality is still around as a relic of bygone days.

The modern church, however, exists as a minority group, an army of revolution seeking to influence centers of power by direct and indirect action. It is rather like an army. Picture an army which builds huge headquarters and spacious training camps, so attractive that the troops prefer to stick around, and the staff want them there anyway because tending the plant requires more and more personnel. Only a few zealous and militant types carry on the battle, out on the frontier. At regular intervals they come home on furlough and give pep talks and illustrated lectures on what soldiering is really like. Then a collection is taken up for the purchase of new equipment and the care of prisoners of war. Would not this be an intolerable situation in wartime? Even in peacetime the build-up of noncombatant personnel is carefully watched, although sometimes the unbalance is amazing. But for the church to tolerate a philosophy of the congregation as a ghetto where one may retreat from the world and assist the clergymen in making things more beautiful, more active (for members only) and more sophisticated—this is intolerable; yet it happens all the time. So our stewardship equation remains incomplete: things do not add up to stewardship but to religious cosiness and self-hypnotism. "At present the life of the congregation, with of course

some exceptions, is neither full nor adult, neither responsible nor corporate. Its present organization prevents it
from being any of these." [6]

Structured for Service

Our congregational activities usually mirror the community and cultural groupings: interest groups, competitive societies, divisive entities. The current Canadian
church problem of uniting two women's organizations (the
Marthas and the Marys) is an example of the point. Perhaps a new orientation of the congregational midweek
activities is needed. The "house church" experiments suggest one way, in which the entire congregation is gathered
in cells for study and action, united through the ministry
of the laity and the goal of service. These activities must
be integrated with the Sunday service, or they do not constitute essential congregational acts. For instance, how
often do clergymen try to avoid "announcements" during
the worship service, because they consider the weekly
activities not "spiritual?" If certain doings are an embarrassing subject for pulpit reference, they should not be
allowed on the premises: that also is part of corporate
stewardship.

But more seriously, all congregational activity should be
so related to service that it is fitting and necessary that it
should have a place in the worship. Incidentally, it was
the custom of most former ages for the preacher to speak
quite naturally about the congregational and community
activities, often before the sermon. Why not *end* the sermon with announcements about the life and work of the
congregation and the community at large? "These announcements ought to receive such a liturgical stamp and
such a particular place in the worship service that they
waken the congregation to an active feeling of responsibility for these cases." [7] They could serve as transition

from sermon to intercession, bringing realism and content into both. Especially they would focus liturgy on service, as its proper issue and consequence.

A further aspect of corporate stewardship is implicit in the radical scriptural meaning of diaconate. Service to the neighbor means more than care for his physical needs. It involves proclamation, witness, and also helping him to love his enemies. It therefore steps right into the controversial areas of community life, with God's Word about the meaning of our life together. It thus provides a context and spur for new thought and new action in its community. If God's grace is surprising, our love should be ingenious, finding new ways to serve. Especially it should be a parable, an acted parable or dramatic representation, of what life together really means. We serve in the Christian sense when we offer this new thing to our neighbors, the radical care and the riotous love of men set free from bondage to fear and self-interest.

If stewardship means seeking to meet human need, then what does modern man "need" most of all? It is surely the integrating power of the gospel, the reality of unity in life and goods, the responsible brotherhood of a group that cares. The congregation must be structured for this kind of service: all its activity, especially its Christian education program, must be a training in nonconformity, a preparation for rebellion, an instruction in the strategy of this surprising love. Otherwise it slips back into the sociologists' picture, blends into the community background, and is a sign only of its human nature.

Serving the Community

Corporate stewardship on the congregational level means a group structured for service, ordered by the goal of serving the community in love.

The servant is one who has become expert in caring, in living for others, in obedience and self-offering. He is one who has learned to make others' good his own. Again and again his life is bent into the shape of someone else's need. He becomes poor so that others may become rich. . . . This life shape, which is the very form of God's own Son, is what Christian ministry means. . . . The only sanctity that matters finally is stewardship and serviceability. On Christian terms there is no eminence of soul which is not also a humbling of self to the dimensions of the cross. . . .[8]

God has matched "the mystery of the poor and the ministry of the rich," [9] so that our service takes the shape of identification with those whom we serve. One is a deacon; that is, one serves Christ both in worship and in care for the neighbor. If one had to choose—sometimes one does!—he would have to choose the latter, even as Christ explicitly states that one serves him in the person of the hungry, the naked, the imprisoned. So it was that the great preacher Chrysostom said, "This altar thou mayest see everywhere lying in lanes and in market places, and thou mayest sacrifice upon it every hour. When thou seest a poor brother, reflect that thou beholdest an altar." [10] The shape of Christ's own service to the Father was sacrificial, crucified love. He poured out his life, until it belonged altogether to others, a ransom for the many. How can our stewardship match that?

The congregational budget may well be the decisive sign of such stewardship. The principle of "one for one," or equal proportion of funds devoted to causes outside the local church, is the best way of signifying this loving service of the neighbor. It may be only a beginning, but it is a good beginning. The congregation can act toward the wider world only through monetary means. Support of the missionary, the fraternal worker in the younger churches, the social worker in the inner city—thus the budget be-

comes the long arm of love. Corporate stewardship shows
its strength here, where the individual can do little on his
own. Just as human needs are institutionalized in this mass
age, so is the power to help, the means of caring. The
money we spend on ourselves is a means of providing adequate provision for worship and training, and unless it is
matched by money for mission, what we do in church becomes perverse and selfish. A 1961 survey of the leading
American denominations showed only 18 per cent of funds
going to "benevolences." This will not do: here the trum-
pet gives an uncertain sound; indeed, here the "house of
prayer" looks like a "den of thieves," and stewardship
becomes a form of robbery!

Moreover, motivation for spending on the local plant is
bound to be a mixed sign, since it partakes of the self-
serving rationale of the average group which benefits us
and our children. Indeed, our congregational canvass
shows the mixed motives clearly enough in its appeal ("the
blessings you miss may be your own"). But motivation for
mission provides a simpler sign for the world to read, since
it indicates an orientation toward others. It shouts aloud
that the business of the Church is not itself but the world
in its need. It thus proclaims the good news that the world
is loved by God, actively loved in its chaos and confusion.
It backs up what is said by the color of its money. It incorporates its service in the very structure of its organized
life and the aim of all its endeavors. It celebrates the
gospel by its joy in serving and its freedom in ordering its
activities by the needs of men. It is therefore a corporate
steward, a congregation that may well be termed Christ's
Body in this place.

Notes for Chapter 5

1. See *Institutionalism and Church Unity*, Nils Ehrenstrom and Walter G. Muelder, eds. (New York: Association Press, 1963). Prepared by the Study Commission on Institutionalism, of the World Council of Churches, it is an indispensable tool in thinking through ecclesiology today.
2. See Paul Broadhurst, "Ecclesiological Themes in the Liturgy Constitution," *The Ecumenist*, May–June, 1964.
3. *The Place of Bonhoeffer*, Martin E. Marty, ed. (New York: Association Press, 1962), Chapter 3. Peter Berger has pointed out that Bonhoeffer's choice of sociological model is not a happy one, so that his work cannot provide a model for others, but only an example of the strength and weakness of such activity. For further thinking on the subject see Bonhoeffer's 1933 lecturers, "Christologie," *Gesammelte Schriften, Band III* (Munich: Chr. Kaiser Verlag, 1960).
4. Categories of "coinherence" are used in contemporary ecclesiology for this pair: "without confusion or separation." E.g., Hans Dombois, "The Church as Koinonia and Institution," *Institutionalism and Church Unity, op. cit.*, pp. 105–122.
5. See the excellent section in Helge Brattgård, *God's Stewards* (Minneapolis: Augsburg Publishing House, 1963), pp. 106ff; also McLelland, "The Challenge of Liturgy," in *Stewardship Explorations* (New York: Ryerson Press, 1963), pp. 111ff.
6. Gibbs and Morton, *God's Frozen People* (New York: Fontana Books, 1964), p. 118.
7. Brattgård, *op. cit.*, p. 198.
8. Roger Hazelton, "Ministry as Servanthood," *The Christian Century*, Apr. 24, 1963. Copyright 1963 Christian Century Foundation. Reprinted by permission.
9. A. Biéler, *La Pensée Economique et Sociale de Calvin* (Geneva: 1954), p. 306.
10. *Hom. XX* on II Corinthians 9:10–LNPNF, Vol. XII, p. 374.

Questions for Discussion

1. Why do church people regard buildings the measure of success in the life of the congregation?
2. Does representative government function well in the average congregation? Why?
3. Who makes the decision in the typical congregation regarding the money sent to do Christian work outside the parish?

4. What is the distinction between "foreign" missions and "home" missions? Between missions "inside" the parish and "outside"?
5. Since so many decisions are made in groups today, what is the place of individual stewardship?
6. What is the role of the individual in the congregation, the labor union, the political party?

6

The Denomination

CHURCH history teaches us that the rise of denominationalism was largely accidental. The early Church knew
variety, but did not institutionalize its diverse forms as we
have today. The religious orders of the medieval Church
represent a significant parallel, with rivalry and waste and
all the problems of bureaucracy. At the time of the Reformation, there was no intention to organize separate denominations; indeed it was a common assumption of the
Reformers that all were united in re-forming the visible
Church.

Archbishop Cranmer, for instance, considered it a simple matter to send invitations to all the leading Reformers
to come to England for a "godly synod"—and those who
came represented diverse theological viewpoints. Through
a number of historical causes, however, some theological
and some political, separate groups were formed, although
in general no two occupied the same territory. It was not
until the settlement of the new world that there developed
the coexistent denominationalism which forms our modern
situation. Now to say that the origins of the problem can
be termed historical accident is not to make its solution

109

any easier. But it serves in a preliminary way to remind us that the current definition "all in each place" deserves a sincere hearing.

The tension between denominational and ecumenical concerns is not our immediate subject, but it is most significant for corporate stewardship. It is a commonplace that one by-product of the ecumenical movement has been the resurgence of denominationalism, through facing the separated groups with questions about their traditions and beliefs. The ironical development has given new life to international bodies that seemed destined to die by a gradual erosion of interest and goals. It has made us all the more conscious of our history, more anxious to preserve denominational heritage and what is sometimes called our "distinctive witness." But it has also produced a new rationalization of certain questionable features of denominational activity. In theology, for example, the study in institutionalism made by the World Council of Churches warned: "Claiming to find a normative church order in the New Testament, it conveniently rediscovers the exact counterpart of that church order in the scholar's own denomination—thereby overlooking the brittleness of the evidence and the diversity and fluidity of the forms in which the early community expressed its life in Christ." [1]

Every group has such defense mechanism, with its theologians the masters of strategy. But something else is evident too. In polity, liturgy, theology, there are signs that old lines are being replaced by more horizontal lines cutting across all denominations, promising at least a better spirit of harmony. The new situation is illustrated best by the recent experience of the Anglican communion, most significant for our theme of corporate stewardship. The Anglican Congress of 1963, held in Toronto, heard its executive officer, Stephen Bayne, declare that the vocation of the Anglican church is to "disappear," as the ecumenical

movement comes to maturity. The blessings peculiar to
Anglicanism must be given to the coming catholic church
without reservation. That was a high moment in denominational stewardship, and it issued in the declaration of
"Mutual Responsibility and Interdependence in the Body
of Christ."

For example, in the total church situation, "The full
communion in Christ which has been our traditional tie
has suddenly taken on a totally new dimension. It is now
irrelevant to talk of 'giving' and 'receiving' churches. The
keynotes of our time are equality, interdependence, mutual responsibility." However, that is easier said than done!
Anglicans are discovering that a second movement is on
foot, apparently the work of many who cannot accept the
disappearing act proposed by Bishop Bayne. A new
bureaucracy seems to be in the making, growing and settling just as Professor Parkinson could have foretold. The
dilemma is clearer for Anglicanism because of the bold
step taken in 1963 and the resulting debate; but it obtains
for us all.

Denominationalism

The phenomenon of denominationalism needs some illuminating distinction. It is not enough to claim a separation
—that it is simply a good thing (since unity is "only spiritual") or simply a bad thing (because disunity is "completely sinful"). The Evanston Assembly suggested such a
distinction, to break the old separation. "Divisions in the
Church have been caused and are perpetuated, to a large
degree, by sincere concern for the gospel." [2] The East-
West schism, the Reformation, decisions about historic
episcopacy and freedom from the state, are examples cited.
But then: "We ask each other whether we do not sin when
we deny the sole lordship of Christ over the Church by

claiming the vineyard for our own, by possessing our 'church' for ourselves, by regarding our theology, order, history, nationality, etc., as our own 'valued treasures,' thus involving ourselves more and more in the separation of all." Here is the question posed by corporate stewardship: is a denomination truly steward of God's mysteries when it witnesses (by definition!) to only part of the church—that is, to a "distinctive witness" which in effect un-churches the others? When this happens, then, as has been said more lately, "the scandal of disunity has been institu-tionalized."

Here is where the sociological analysis applies to de-nomination as well as to congregation. If it is true that "more than doctrine divides the churches," are the non-theological factors a help or a hindrance in stewardship? For example, the author of this chapter belongs to a de-nomination which prides itself on having the Church of Scotland for its mother, which fosters an image of being "the Kirk" within Canada, and which reflects a Celtic cul-ture symbolized by Burns' Suppers, Iona Chapels, and folklore about Covenanters. Is such a church able to break out of this ethnic domestication? Is its "distinctive wit-ness" that of a really "free" church and a really "reform-ing" church? It is not alone, of course, for we all operate with group values and norms and myths.

In the first place, therefore, corporate stewardship de-mands of the denomination that it examine its relation to the ecumenical movement, that its distinctive witness be constantly evaluated in the light of the changing scene, and that competition between denominations—especially in that rich territory of suburbia—be rooted out com-pletely. The world is not deceived by our verbal statements about our underlying unity, when they witness our un-seemly and wasteful duplication of personnel and funds in surveys and new buildings. "All in each place" must mean something soon or it too will become another slogan invented by idealists and buried by realists.

A Question of Institutionalism

The humanity of the Church, open as it is to sociological analysis, reminds us that in polity, structure, organization, the church participates in all the good and bad things that "institutionalism" has come to mean today. Why is it we think that everything done in the church is holy? Insofar as the church is an institution, it is a power structure, a bit of humanity characterized by the interpersonal relations which reflect the tension, the image making (there's a theological note!) and role playing familiar to us all in theory and in experience. It is also plagued by the "institutionalized indecision" which committees engender, the lack of mobility and decisiveness typical of bureaucracy. Committees, of course, are notoriously questionable means of getting anything done: "a group of the unready appointed by the unwilling to do the unnecessary." For these reasons, the denomination needs constantly to evaluate its structure in terms of institutional and technical renovation; that is a fundamental of its stewardship, both to economize in personnel and funds, and to organize itself better to fulfill the mission of the Church.

We are not speaking only of the denominational executive here, although necessarily he is the man. Canonical or constitutional power in the church is of little effect unless harnessed to administrative power. Power resides in the office rather than in the person, in church as in state. The emphasis of the denominational stewardship program will depend largely on the structures of power discernible within its head office. Boards and agencies inevitably function as rivals for the funds available from the total budget. The natural conflict among such boards is probably heightened by the ideological fact that an ecclesiastical agent tends to be totalitarian in his claims. The whole range of church activity and goal can be summed up under "mission"—or "Christian education"—or "evangelism"—or even "stewardship"! And in one sense each of these divisions can make a reasonably good case. They are divided not because there are such divisions in reality, but only to provide some practical way to do the total work by human agencies.

Yet within the church headquarters, how familiar is the struggle for power, the rivalry and jockeying for position![3] It is so easy to be a server of statistical returns, or—here is the peculiar temptation of all stewardship bureaucrats!—a slave of the mimeograph machine. The "real church" becomes the head office and its little group of professional workers, and all the congregations are the hewers of wood and drawers of water to keep this central plant going.

Power and Pressure

The question is, how does this institutional situation affect the total mission of the Church? Is the denominational budget loaded in the direction of glorifying the image of its "distinctive witness," for instance? Does it indulge in a "denominational ecumenism" which pretends to be truly catholic but which is a form of imperialism? To be sure, as Allport's studies have shown, there need be no ultimate clash between "concentric loyalties," if denominational and ecumenical loyalties are geared together. But does the denominational executive attempt to do this, at the risk of jeopardizing his image as a custodian of the received tradition? For various reasons one does not expect to find radicals in administrative positions, yet the executive can foster the radical spirit throughout his denomination by his stewardship of power, if this is guided by the mission we have indicated above.

Power means pressure. There are the pressures upon the executive himself, from the denomination—usually a pressure to conserve and entrench and safeguard, and another to expand the institution, to enhance its image, to validate its continuing existence. Then there are the pressures which the executive can apply, through emphases in its literature and publicity and budgetary decisions and personnel deployment. The result will be a complex yet true humanity by which the denomination fulfills the goals it considers its own.

While we are still on the more negative aspects of institutionalism, we should note a particularly sinister form of pressure which has arisen in relation to the younger churches of the world. We are so used to "missionary imperialism" that we still have not recognized the extent to which "he who pays the piper calls the tune." We began to suspect it some years ago when spokesmen for the younger churches of the East told us bluntly that they would not accept our interpretation of (European) church history—do not give us your Western divisions, so they phrased it. To someone who assumes that to be a Christian means to accept a quite Lutheran concept of justification by faith alone or a quite Calvinist concept of divine sovereignty, for instance, that hits below the theological belt.

Lately there have been suggestions that just as our Western theology comes from the mating of Hebrew thought with Greek, so theirs might conceivably develop from a new encounter of Hebrew thought with Indian or Chinese or African.[4] What should our denominations do with these willful offspring? Do they deserve our financial support? Don't they know that we are their mother churches? Where would they be without us? Even worse is the fact that in administration—that means, in the spending of our money!—they demand complete self-determination, and accept our personnel only as "fraternal workers." Will our denominations discover sufficient resources of Christian love to support the younger churches, regardless of what strange new ways their theology and polity and liturgy may take? And will our denominations prove resilient enough to learn new things for their own growth in grace and knowledge, that all may truly be one?

Redeemed Principalities and Creative Powers

"All power corrupts," even ecclesiastical power. We struggle against the corrupting and perverting tendency of power even when this means the church in its institutionalized form. Christ has effected the victory over all principalities and powers, in his death and resurrection.[5] Power in the church is not by definition holy, as we have stated already, yet it is in the best position to show what a redeemed power is like. It is a superpersonal structure, with a dynamic all its own, so that when it is corrupted it represents evil in an abnormally sinister form (anti-Christ?).

And conversely, when it is good it represents Christ's grace at work in a particularly potent form. The critique of institutionalism should not blind us to the positive fact that we need structure: structures of evil must be met by structures of good, as Paul Tillich has put it. Was it not a primary insight of the social gospel, thanks to Rauschenbusch, that sin and grace may be predicated of such principalities as well as of individuals?

The denomination dedicated to mission is a redeemed principality which produces good in the world. Every polity has its peculiar vice, its form of bureaucracy; yet some institutional form is inescapable (for theological as well as practical reasons). Our task is to help our denominations recognize their call to corporate stewardship, to spell out positive and specific tasks by which their power may be used creatively. This is not to make any value judgment about the validity of denominations as such. The concept of "all in each place" means that denominational division manifests a disunity at local levels and in practical affairs which must be judged evil, a denial of stewardship.

If the most flagrant evils are mitigated through sensible comity agreements or mutual recognition of ministries and so on, then perhaps one could agree to a relative stability. But it would seem that denominationalism itself is on the spot today, and the call is to obedience unto death, to a bold step toward new forms of our common life together. In this deeper sense, the corporate stewardship of denominations, if properly attempted, will itself force the ecumenical question. For if all denominations are re-forming themselves toward goals of Christ's one mission to the world, they will draw toward the center, which is Christ himself, and so toward one another.

Pure Research

By "creative power" we mean to say that the denomination must adventure beyond the safe waters of traditional goals and patterns. Something new must emerge from its stewardship, signifying the presence of the living God and the effects of his surprising grace. If the old parish grouping is no longer a relevant structure, for instance, then instead of trying desperately to renew it, the administration should be encouraging experiment in para-parochial forms. As one inner city worker has challenged: "Rather than attacking and defending present church structures let the denominations take some of the most talented young rebels and explore today's world. The young men who are so critical of present institutions must produce some models of ministry that focus on God's missionary activity in the world."[6] There must be radical reappraisal of our traditional pattern: inner city, campus, industry, business, and downtown. And there must be dialogue between, so that the common ministry is not divided within itself.

Such experimentation, however, is almost entirely dependent on denominational resources and administrative decisions. It is like the "pure research" work financed by visionary foundations or farsighted industrial firms. Much of it will lead nowhere, but some of it will discover the pathways of the future. So corporate stewardship for the denomination means doing that which no congregation can do for itself yet which every congregation deserves to have: new models of ministry provided by funds diverted through executive initiative.

If significant sums are invested in experimental forms of ministry, the denomination will be offering that service peculiar to it as an institution. It will thus be a pace setter for all its membership, and will in turn challenge them in their stewardship to follow the growing edge of search and research into new forms of being the Church. It may well be that the Church should be found on the side of more lost causes than it likes to be, in behalf of witness to Christ. This is not to advocate a theology of failure, but to question the image of the successful church which we all serve these days. The "OK" church in an "OK" world may suit our affluent society, but it looks as ludicrous as it sounds to serious men who seek solutions for twentieth-century problems of war and hunger and apathy. If the program of interchurch aid and refugee relief were pursued more heartily, a sign for our times could be erected for all to see; for is not the denomination, like the individual Christian, called to an ethic characterized by what

John C. Bennett has termed "the aggressive care for marginal cases"?

The larger the group, the greater its care program and the more effective its love. We seem anxious, however, to keep love on the individual level, while the denomination concentrates on "church extension." Stewardship at this stage brings the same test as faces the congregation: an equal proportion of funds spent outside its own constituency, or at least a proportionate spread in direct and indirect ways of fulfilling our mission at home and abroad. We cannot demand a new kind of tithe—one-half instead of one-tenth—but we can insist on a show of service with the cost written in. As the Anglican *Mutual Responsibility* declaration put it: "We need to examine our priorities, asking whether in fact we are not putting secondary needs of our own ahead of essential needs of our brothers."

Public Morality

How does the Church speak to the world today? With the passing of Christendom went the direct influence and authoritative office which was known and accepted by the civil community. Today the denomination tends to rely on official pronouncements of its administrative body to comment on public issues. Congregations and subgroups usually leave it to the larger to speak for them. More lately, the ministry of the laity has meant that churches recognize the need to help their laymen speak *as the Church* within the world. Since we are concerned with the denomination here, we shall take the latter for granted, and insist that the denomination fulfill its corporate stewardship when it assumes its role as spokesman to the nation. It is the denominational voice which will influence government, public morality, political economy. Let us look briefly at each of these three in turn.

Politicians know that statistics count; how large a seg-
ment of the constituency does this lobby group represent?
Official pronouncements may seem a safe way of showing
"concern" without the involvement of responsibility. Yet,
as a denomination, it is one thing the institution owes its
national community. Indeed, here it may function as
the Congregation (similar to those civic "Lords of the
Congregation" in Reformed Scotland) speaking to its community—the national congregation addressing its immediate locality. How ecumenism raises its head at every turn,
however! Surely genuine stewardship demands that the
denomination follow its logic and seek a united front with
other denominations in the land when addressing the government. It is hard to see how the usual time, talent, and
treasure of stewardship apply to the denomination, but in
our present reference we may say that a lead should be
given to its member congregations in the use of all three to
support the government in its good causes and to protest
in its bad. This distinction is vital to stewardship, for what
the Church owes the state is not blind obedience but responsible and creative citizenship.

Public morality is the traditional sphere of denominational stewardship. In fact, the negative mood of official
pronouncements about alcoholic beverages and gambling
and Sunday observance and sexual license makes up the
image of how the Church speaks to the nation. Besides,
the churches have relied on a variety of agencies or voluntary societies to keep tab on each of these, like watchdogs
on a leash. The typical church pronouncement is expected
to be "against sin and for motherhood." Now we should
not like simply to reverse the terms! But the old idea of
morality was the product of an individual bourgeois culture which tended to reduce ethics to simple terms within
the private sphere of life. Social causes were played down,
and the upright citizen was sketched in ascetic tones of

black and white. The complexity of ethical norms, the whole sweep of social ethics indeed, was virtually unrecognized. This still obtains in more conservative ecclesiastical circles, where issues of personal morality are considered central, and the public sphere left to the devil. Here, then, is where the denomination has to recover sounder theological insights about its stewardship to the nation. It owes a more positive and constructive and socially realistic critique of public morality. It owes this on behalf of, and in the name of, the God who created the world, its things, and its people, and saw how good it was; how much better even it can become in Christ.

"Employee" Society

Political economy has already suggested itself as relevant for moral issues. Does not our stewardship teaching suffer in missing the point here? We begin too far along the way, after people have earned their money, and we tell them how to distribute it. Should we not, for the sake of good stewardship, say something about the making of it? P. T. Forsyth once stated the point in a powerful way: "Simple personal faith will not of itself give the power and insight to apply the Christian moral principle to the accepted standards of the age. As a matter of fact, such faith has had more effect on the disposal of wealth than on the moral making of it. Some of the truest believers are harassed by the way they are involved in an egoist system of accumulation. And how many more are mammonized by it!" [7]

Could not the denomination take the lead in attacking this problem, by bending its stewardship program to push back into the arena of property and work, of commerce and finance, of business and industry? If ours is an "employee" society in which everyone works for some corporation, cannot this ecclesiastical corporation speak a word of good cheer and be itself a sign of hope? (By the way, how many denominations pay their office staff a living wage, and provide adequate working conditions?)

The denomination is ideally situated to examine the political economy of its national community in order to probe its assumptions, its ethos, and its consequences. So afraid are we of endorsing one political party or one economic theory as against another that we refuse to comment on the subject at all. This is not good stewardship. It denies the clear fact that there are moral implications of every theory and practice of political economy. To play at being neutral, of course, is really to support the status quo—as the church usually does. Is there not a question in stewardship between the view which locates all economic incentive in the profit motive, and that which seeks other motivation? Or between rival theories (for example, "structuralist" and "generalist") of the cause and cure of unemployment and how manpower is to be used? Political economy is the management of the common wealth—the public household. It is itself, therefore, a sort of secular stewardship. As with every human discipline, it operates with certain theories or "models."

Surely our Christian stewardship is a model with some relevance to the civil community! The Church has a long history of teaching on economics which contains at least one principle needed today: "Production is on account of consumption" (St. Antonino). There is a qualifier to put to our society's model! For we consume on account of production, with finance playing a new role as the power élite of the business community. If the Church were to develop its social ethics today as zealously as our fathers did their personal ethics, we should have plenty to say to modern society—and it would listen![8]

The Stewardship Program

The denomination creates the program of stewardship for its congregations, providing instruction, encouragement, and direction. In this area it is the key, setting the tone for all its congregations and members. Here is where the same bureaucracy so criticized by us all may function as a good steward, pushing forward into new territory and bringing its denomination to greater service for the glory of God. "Benevolence promotion" is still associated in most minds with "the needs of the church," that is, the group goals for its own future. The keynote of mission must be more boldly sounded through all church programs so that it will be clear that by "churchly needs" we mean, in fact, "for serving the *world* better." Stewardship is still too institution centered, oriented about the challenges of an expanding population, a changing society, and consequent modifications in churchly ways. It must by its emphases and methods become more of a teaching arm by which the Church brings its membership to a missionary condition. If stewardship really is for mission, then benevolence promotion needs not only to change its name but to breathe a more fiery spirit of challenge and crisis.

The "Money" Sword

Do we realize the image we create in the world's eyes by our approach to financing? The manner of our stewardship is itself one of the chief signs by which we witness to the kind of God we really serve. We are not promoting only the schemes of the denomination when we engage in this activity, but the gospel itself, which is judged by its fruits among us. I wonder how we react to the comment of that peculiar prophet, Roland Allen, known for his trenchant analysis of missionary methods fifty years ago. About stewardship he once said: "Another age may learn to look upon our use of activities much as we look upon the use of the sword by an earlier age. Because in them money takes so prominent a place, ours may one day be known as the age of financial Christianity, just as we look upon that earlier age as the age of military Christianity. As we regard the sword so a later age may regard money. It may learn the wisdom of the apostle and decline to use such an ambiguous weapon. If the sword was an ambiguous weapon which might easily confuse the issue, money, and activities which depend upon money, are not less ambiguous and may as easily confuse the issue. The time is not yet ripe. We have yet to learn the consequences of our use of money." [9]

A similar comment from the Church of Rome is also relevant to this point, since it indicates a more cautious attitude toward church financing than is common among us. It is by a man named Montini, now Pope Paul VI. Speaking about special "days" for collections for the church, he stated: "They show our poverty, the honor of the Church today, which forces us to suffer and to beg for works and plans that our ministry cannot abandon. . . . It is well that we understand this fact: The Church always lacks resources proportionate to its mission. The Church is forbidden secular activity for economic gain. In this hour when others are affluent, the Church is passing through a critical period of growing needs with absolutely insufficient resources with which to meet them. It is here that our hope quickens, not only for our own profit and comfort but for the benefit of all good works, that the hour of economic affluence may become the hour of charity. In this way it may also become the hour of justice and peace." [10]

Both comments remind us that there is more than one quality of expectation in stewardship, perhaps more than one kind of "spirituality" moving through this area of promotion and asking and suggesting. Have we hardened our theology of stewardship too soon, pleased with the results of our businesslike methods and realistic approach? Would we do the same in a depressed economy? If not, then what elements now important might be expendable? These are questions which other churches and, not least, younger churches, are already asking us. If it is the denominational executive who sets the pace in stewardship, then his is the responsibility to break new ground here also, and to surprise us with something new.

NOTES FOR CHAPTER 6

1. *The Old and the New in the Church* (Minneapolis: Augsburg Publishing House, 1961), p. 76. Used by permission.
2. *Evanston Speaks* (Geneva: WCC, 1954), Report of Section 1: "Our Oneness in Christ and Our Disunity as Churches," p. 14.
3. See Walter Muelder, "Problems of Church Bureaucracy" in *Institutionalism and Church Unity*, p. 158: "Operational agency roles may overrule inclusive Christian vocation. Missions may thwart mission, and the unit may block unity."
4. For example, "The Forthcoming Role of the Non-Christian Religious Systems as Contributory to Christian Theology," Herbert C. Jackson, *Missionary Research Library Occasional Bulletin*, March 15, 1961; *cf.* the "Christian Presence Series" published by SCM.
5. Since we cannot go into the detailed theology of this subject here, we refer you to a stimulating preparatory study, "Christians in Power Structures," in the *Laity* bulletin for Nov., 1962.
6. Don Benedict, "Structures for the New Era," *Renewal* (Chicago City Missionary Society), Oct., 1963.
7. Quoted by E. R. Wickham from a lecture delivered in 1905, *Church and People in an Industrial City* (London: Lutterworth Press, 1957), p. 202.
8. *Cf.* on this point, McLelland, "The Challenge of Socialism," in *Stewardship Explorations* (Montreal: Canadian Council of Churches, 1963) pp. 132ff.
9. Quoted by Paul van Buren in "Stewardship—an Ecumenical Confrontation," *Laity*, Oct., 1961, p. 65.

10. G. B. Montini, *The Christian in the Material World* (Montreal: Palm Publishers, 1963), p. 65.

QUESTIONS FOR DISCUSSION

1. Who makes the key decisions in your denomination? Board members? How are they elected?
2. How is a denomination like a civil government? Parties? Patronage? Bureaucracy?
3. Is denominational pride a factor in the placement of new congregations?
4. What denominational agency is best equipped to handle endowments?

7

The Nation

AT midtwentieth century something new has happened to nationalism. It has become a thing of the past, no longer fit for the future. Yet nationalism not only continues but grows in power, as it captivates the new and emerging nations freed from colonialism. We must approach the idea of corporate stewardship as applied to the nation, therefore, in terms appropriate to this paradox.

What has made nationalism outdated? Not the visionary expectation of Marxism that in due process of revolution and evolution the State would atrophy; Russia itself, for instance, shows striking characteristics of nationalism. In a word, the change has been effected by The Bomb. Let us define the nation as the "survival unit," the group united as a competitive entity distinct from other groups. There are other ways of defining nation, chiefly in terms of political economy, but our modern situation results from the change in strategies of survival, beside which these others become secondary. The evolution of society has witnessed the general growth of the survival unit from family or clan to city-state, and finally, nation. But now, how are things with us? Let me quote from one of the best exponents of the point, Brock Chisholm, former director general, World

Health Organization: "Quite suddenly the survival-unit has become not the family, the tribe, the clan, the city-state, the principality, nor even the nation, but the human race itself. A situation has now arisen where no group can defend itself against deadly attack from outside. The old competitive survival to the death has now become synonymous with racial suicide."[1]

We are the first generation capable of committing racial suicide: that capability is the formative element in corporate stewardship today. Old ways of living together in groups are of little help in this new situation, since they were formed by a philosophy of intergroup competition, a struggle for survival whose ultimate weapon was the ability and willingness to eliminate the opposing group if necessary. That ultimate has been removed: the ridiculous concept of "overkill" reminds us that we passed it some time ago. We either learn to live together as a racial unit (I mean race in the proper sense of "human race" and not the improper myth of subgroups called "races"), an international human family—or we plan to die together as an international human family. The Bomb has indeed made us familial! Perhaps it is time our churches started beginning their stewardship promotion with a word about this corporate stewardship of nuclear power, instead of leaving all that to their social action committees or to the ecclesiastical beatniks on the left fringe.

Control of Creation

Let us be clear about the implications of our new situation. It calls in question the whole idea of nationalism as this has developed among us, especially in the West in the past five hundred years. It cannot simply necessitate a new international structure, or institutionalize the oneness of humanity in some supernational world order. That may well have to be considered; but meanwhile the situation is too new, and the adjustment too painful. The governing idea must be one of "united nations"—that is, of nations still, but oriented about a different purpose.

We need "planned nationhood" geared to master the technological and ideological dynamics of our unified world. The oneness achieved forcibly and dramatically by nuclear power is but a symptom of the truth of our oneness in human nature and destiny. We have been evolving toward this control of "nature" through the millennia behind us, as the ancient myth taught us in its description of man as lord over the animal kingdom, and steward of the earth itself (Genesis 1:28–29, 2:15–19). Now we have reached the pinnacle of evolution: the power to halt the process itself. Julian Huxley has familiarized us with this idea of the new stage in human history which is upon us, and in the thought of Teilhard de Chardin we find a significant Christian evaluation.

As scientist and theologian, archeologist and traveler, de Chardin became convinced that our century's achievements represent a breakthrough, a decisive step forward in our destiny, which he termed the entry into the "noussphere," the layer of reality governed by mind. But he also gained another insight, less erudite but perhaps more helpful. In a conversation he was once asked the secret of his joyful nature. "Why am I happy?" he replied. "Because the earth is round." Life on a round planet implies unity, fellowship; there are no corners or edges where some may live in isolation. It is part of the history of nationalism that such isolation (we call it "autonomy" or "sovereignty of the state") is the foundation of things.

It was the Great War which symbolized the end of the old nationalism; think of the heart searching of America before the decision to send its army "over there"! But now there is no longer any faraway place, any alien soil. The roundness of the planet suggests the shape of humanity itself—bound together on a sphere which limits yet which offers an infinity of space. There is no "end" to the movement of the human family over this globe, if it will learn to use its freedom in the service of humanity as a whole.

"National self-interest" is no longer sufficient to justify the actions of a state: it must appear before the bar of "the universal commonweal." [2] Every national economy, for instance, represents a self-centered philosophy: tariff scales, immigration laws, even the rationale of assisting underdeveloped nations—all betray the isolationist and selfish assumptions we take for granted. The nation exists to serve its own citizens in their quest for higher living standards as the absolute goal and determinant; it does not exist to serve the human family. To be sure, the problem here is complex, like that of motivation in the economy. Can one balance and modify the profit motive by other forms of incentive which will prove as fruitful and reliable? That is a similar question to this one about the motivation behind national activities and policies. Both questions involve technical aspects which appear to be genuine "nontheological factors." But both involve a philosophy of human nature and destiny which poses a challenge to the church, especially in its theology of stewardship.

Church and State

Theology tends to be a conservative, often reactionary, discipline. It was shaped in the patristic era so powerfully that we find it difficult to do more than add commentary. This is true not only in the more obvious points of Chalcedonian-Nicene trinitarian doctrine, but also in the teaching on man and his behavior. New insights in the latter realm take time to sink in. In ethics, for instance, we still tend to operate with ancient categories of a self-determining individual in an environment which he controls or to which he is equal. The need for realism about the dominant and willful nature of power structures in the modern world is still confined to prophetic spirits. Think of Reinhold Niebuhr, as early as 1932 warning us about the strange situation of "moral man and immoral society." One of his illustrations is relevant today, when the U.S.A. seems ready to "liberate" Cuba by force of arms: "The Spanish-American War offers some of the most striking illustrations of the hypocricy of governments as well as of the self-deception of intellectuals. . . . We decided to keep the Philippines against their will at the conclusion of a war ostensibly begun to free the Cubans."[3] It is in this realm of "hypocrisy" and "self-deception" that theology must modify the old doctrine of "church and state."

Traditionally, we have thought of the church-state relationship in terms of the model provided by Christendom. Here was an established church—that is, recognized and accepted by the government as necessary to society's well-being—functioning as the religious aspect of the total group. The church could well take itself seriously as the "conscience of the nation," for when it spoke, especially in its official pronouncements, the state listened—and often obeyed! Today that is either gone completely or going fast. In the majority of nations the church is either a competitor in a pluralistic religious situation, or is the nonconformist sect where a non-Christian religion is the established church.

In a minority of nations (almost exclusively in the West) the church is still the "religious aspect" of the group, "the nation at prayer," but is no longer listened to with much seriousness. Of course, the church fools itself into thinking it counts for something because it hears so many powers invoking the name of the deity in critical situations. Surely we understand how dangerous that game

is, from the amusing documentation of what could be
called "Eisenhower" religion, provided by writers like Will
Herberg, Martin Marty, and Peter Berger! Belief in God-
in-general, or having faith in faith, is a sign that the church
is *not* being taken seriously. It may mean that the church
has become domesticated, "kept" by the state; or it may
mean that the nation considers the church only a historical
manifestation of religion in general. In either case the
church is in a new situation, and most of what theologians
still say about church-state relations is nonsense.

The part that is not nonsense is the part that sees in the
political realm a divinely ordained structure. But here one
wonders whether we can rescue the idea from questionable
forms. It is not the nation as such which has God behind
it, but the civil community whatever its particular form,
so long as the form expresses human solidarity, the divine
vocation to be brothers. It is this that the Church has to say
to the state, this part of the good news which illuminates
the civil community as a thing of good. The state is not
called to be the Church, as if it should try to live by norms
of love, by the gospel. It is not love but justice by which
the state is ordered, but such justice as is appropriate to
brotherhood. The fraternal relationship must be encouraged by the civic justice. A graphic illustration of this is
presented in our continent just now by the civil rights
struggle. We do not mean here the part which the Church
has played, or rather which the Church refused to play
until so dangerously late in the game. We refer to another
aspect of the struggle: the place which the law occupies in
human relationships.

Injustice

As the issue of civil rights in the U.S.A. developed toward its climax over the past year or more, government

spokesmen looked to the churches to provide a "favorable climate." Whether they are doing so is difficult to judge. Martin Luther King, Jr., writing from Birmingham Jail, lamented "the appalling silence of the good people . . . the white moderate who is more devoted to 'order' than to justice." [4] In that letter he also scored the familiar argument that segregation is a "local problem" to be solved by "insiders": "I am in Birmingham because injustice is here. . . . Injustice anywhere is a threat to justice everywhere. We are caught in an inescapable network of mutuality, tied in a single garment of destiny. . . ." Although King is speaking for everyone living within America, must the principle not be extended to all mankind? Such a moral issue is everyone's concern, everyone's crisis. This is why it appeals to justice, to the use of law in the hands of men. To what extent can morality be legislated? is one way of stating the question.

Speaking to this very point, a Canadian Dean of Law, Professor Bowker of the University of Alberta, addressing the Canadian Bar Association, said that whatever discrimination remains in Canada has no legal support, whereas the American Constitution may bar discriminatory laws but lacks teeth. "The teeth are provided by legislation that forbids discriminatory acts by individuals or groups," he explained. "The constitutional enactment is a shield, but the victim of discrimination needs a sword as well. . . . Society always uses pressures, non-legal as well as legal, to make its members conform in their conduct . . . one of the roles of law is to operate as an instrument of social control . . . anti-discrimination law does not purport to make the discriminator love the man of different race or color. It merely tells him to treat him as he would anyone else."

No, you cannot legislate love and to that extent you cannot legislate a morality of brotherhood. But you can

govern the behavior of citizens by such legislation as corresponds to the philosophy of human fraternity, the insight
about human nature that underlies the nation's own being.
It is in this sense that the nation is steward of the very
being of its citizens, and requires the support of its Christian citizens in paving the way for legislation which will
guide human behavior in proper treatment of fellow men.
When this is lacking, then democracy is a sham, for all
citizens participate in a tyranny, a climate of unfreedom.
This explains the irony of the civil rights struggle, as expressed by Roy Wilkins, NAACP Secretary, at the civil
rights march in Washington, when he stated that it must
be said to those Southerners who want to vote for the
administration's bill but don't dare: "Just give us a little
time, and one of these days we'll emancipate you."

The irony lies in man's relationship to his neighbor: he
who separates his brother from himself thereby separates
himself from his brother. The real slave was the owner;
the real victim today is the white Southerner, caught in the
trap of his isolation which only the Negro can spring.
Brotherhood, fraternity—this is the secret of a nation's
proper governance of its people's lives and property ("We
hold these truths . . ."). Corporate stewardship at the
national level is not just a question of legislation against
monopolies, but against every manifestation of that hatred
which spells the death of mutual respect and therefore the
death of genuine order in the state.

Decision to Care

If the civil community is faced with a choice in shaping
its justice to the demands of fraternity, then can there not
be decision in every sphere of its life in like terms? That
is to say, the nation can develop its policies through
choices which reveal its basic and essential decision *to
care*. In its domestic policy, this is embodied in legislation

providing adequately for what is generally termed "welfare"—the care of the aged, the sick, the unemployed. So much emotional appeal to "freedom of the individual" has been made (as if this were threatened by the care program of the state) that it is difficult to break through prejudice into a rational approach.

The Church has certainly been a notable failure at this point, especially the Reformed family of churches, where each generation's theologians dedicate themselves to disprove Max Weber's thesis about "the protestant ethic and the spirit of capitalism," while many of its people seem dedicated to its support. Have we nothing better to offer the state than an outdated bourgeois ethic? Must we not point out that when government sets out to care for its marginal cases through legislation and the use of tax revenues, this is not "creeping socialism" or centralization gone wild, but a valid and necessary function? One could suggest parallels in the Old Testament, where "evangelical legislation" shows striking concern for the neighbor, particularly debtors and slaves.[5]

Legislation for the lowly ought to be a clear word which Christ's church always has to speak to the state. Instead, we seem to think we must defend the "rights" of those who possess, and rely on their charity—their "benevolence" or good will!—to provide some measure of relief for those who have not. So concerned with private property have we been that our stewardship asks no questions about how the money was earned, but suggests that if a tithe is given to God, the remainder will increase a hundredfold. Thus a sort of calculus of investment develops—"God runs my business." The so-called "free enterprise" system of political economy becomes sanctified, and in its name we are told that the church must not meddle in political economy! How ironical it is that the Church of Rome has been able to support a proper "socialization" necessary in the modern world (in Pope John XXIII's encyclical *Mater et Magistra*).

The concern for the needy should have place within the national economy, not in terms of charity but in terms of justice. A sign of our times is the current debate in both Canada and the United States concerning "medicare." Those who oppose a national program do so usually on the grounds of freedom, and the responsibility of the individual for his own medical care. But this fails to consider two aspects relevant to our present discussion. One is the fact that such individualism is not consistent with the principle of fraternity, the mutual dependence of the members of the human community. More important is the fact that it is no longer realistic to expect anyone but the rich to afford the resources of physician and hospital now necessary in the care and cure of the sick. In this latter sense, medicare is almost a technical strategy to meet a new situation, and has little philosophical significance.

In the West, of course, we actually have the "welfare state" to some degree or other. Many Canadians, for instance, consider Americans quite socialist in their amazing "Social Security" program! The decisive question in this area, however, has not been asked until we consider what the man who has, *owes* (for example, in tax dollars) to the man who has less. That question is compatible with sound economics, but usually it arises in a context of fraternity; and no doubt it makes for modification of the economy in the direction of legislative care. We are saying, therefore, that the decision to care will affect the national economy much as we suggested that the congregational and denominational budget should be slanted. It will not be a proportionate slant, since the state is not a church; but, if the Church gives guidance, the state may well be spurred to appropriate measures.

Have and Have Nots

The nation needs to be challenged, especially the "moderate" majority of citizens who make decisions effective. The challenge to choose forms of economic justice which care for the needy of the land also needs to be made against the larger background of humanity. Foreign policy cannot be divorced from domestic policy. Consider the terrible fact of the disproportion between defense expenditure and aid to underdeveloped countries. What about "prestige plans" such as the moon race? Is forty billions of American dollars a good investment, presumably matched by similar Russian funds? Is such competition between nations, both in defense and in prestige programs, justifiable in the light of the needs of nonaffluent nations? Or is there a like principle of stewardship involved here to that which we enunciated for denominations?

Take a more telling case: our use—or abuse—of surplus food is surely a scandal for stewardship. Whether it is Canadian wheat bursting our granaries or American potatoes willfully destroyed, it comes to the same thing: we operate on economic principles not good enough for a unified world. Stewardship demands that these principles be scrapped in favor of better ones. Even what we do spend on the underdeveloped nations is conditioned by a selfish rationale: we'd better do it so that they won't become Communists! Our hypocrisy and lack of subtlety in this respect actually accentuate the "have and have not" relationship.

The key to a better stewardship for the nation lies in a better appreciation of power structures in the modern world. Corporate stewardship means *collective* stewardship—the group acting responsibly in view of its corporate power. In the past it has been governmental power that was curbed, on the grounds that authority is always dan-

gerous and control over people is morally wrong. But we
have been reluctant to apply this principle to control over
things, to the power that is given by *property.*

The power structure today is symbolized by the "corporation," and it needs a long, hard look in the light of our
understanding of corporate stewardship.[6] This explains
why it is not sufficient to appeal to government for better
policies in our new situation. We must help the governing
authority lead its "power élite" into new ways of being
responsible. Naturally this will involve legislative measures
to curb and to direct the use of power through property;
for if the analysis of contemporary social science is at all
correct in its claim that the effective decisions in political
economy are made not in government but in business
circles, then realism demands a "corporation stewardship."
When power structures are so mobilized for action toward
the international community, our world will be one step
nearer to the goal of corporate stewardship, the use of this
world's goods for the benefit of all.

British economist Barbara Ward has commented that
for the first time in history we have resources to match
our imagination. Only a few years after the first space
flight, the moon is within our grasp. Therefore the limiting
factor is no longer what resources are available, but what
imagination. We may solve the technical problems of
production in underdeveloped countries, better distribution in affluent societies, remedies for the population ex-
plosion, but unless we solve the greater problem of living
together on our shrunken planet, we shall not have positive direction or worthy goals for our mastery of things.
United action across national boundaries is required for
such a time as this. We are still only on the threshold of
this new way of being a nation; therefore one can but
give signs and suggestions, as we explore the new path,

for if we lose heart and shrink back into the old way of nationhood, we shall not survive in the new age.

The Glory of the Nations

We have said that the nation is no longer the viable survival unit. National sovereignty, in the traditional sense of ability to protect the lives, property, and values of its citizens, is no longer meaningful. Being a nation now means something other than that, something new in our history. It means to exist along with other nations in a larger community, and therefore to exist for the other nations too, to balance one's budget in view of their needs. Nations must plan for a future in which new patterns of international co-operation and action are the rule. They must accept the new condition under which claims of sovereignty are made: the condition imposed by the world community.

One sign of the new time ahead is the current state of international law. What is needed is "the rule of law in the world," according to groups such as the World Federalists, who point out that the United Nations is still subject to the foreign policies of the great powers. The principle of "one nation: one vote" obtains, and the veto power—introduced originally by the United States!—continues to deny the concept of international law. We are facing a crisis in this area which may well prove decisive in the struggle for corporate stewardship. "The sense of a 'crisis' in international law experienced by many observers today is a product of the acceleration of the processes of change in the international community that is characteristic of our era." [7] A world community requires universal law, under which every nation must place itself as one member of this greater "body politic." That will require boldness and sacrifice on the part of all nations—qualities which institutions in general and sovereign states in particular seem to lack!

Yet just what is the genius of a nation? The Bible contains many insights about peoples and nations, and its climax in the Book of Revelation speaks of the "glory" of the nations, which they shall bring into the kingdom of God when it comes (Revelation 21:24–26). May we not expect that the contribution of the various nations to international law and to human fraternity may be exactly what is implied in the concept of "corporate stewardship?" That is, should we not regard old nations and new nations as stewards of their cultures, responsible for handing on— or "handing over"—the fruits of their history to the whole race? Then each would contribute to the greater glory of humanity, not in terms of a simple humanism, but of a Christian humanism attuned to the biblical idea of the glory of the nations. Indeed, in certain ancient cultures there is evidence of insight into the essential unity of mankind which makes our Western gropings seem like child's play. China's philosophy of a unifying cosmic principle, or India's ethical deal of *sarvodaya,* or Africa's "primal vision" in which "stewardship" in brotherly service is basic —have they nothing to say to us in our activistic, individualistic, and theoretical approach to common life? We are able to see only a little of what may come through national decision, because we are accustomed to think of forms of justice and brotherhood within our own cultural possibilities.

Remember Christ's parable about the Lord's vineyard (Matthew 21:33–44)? The tenants had become unworthy stewards because they were not open to the claim of the owner, were not prepared for his word. The solution was simple: the property would go to other tenants, prepared to be stewards. If the kingdom was once taken from the Jews and given to the Church, must not the Church face the possibility that it too may lose it through unworthy tenancy, so that new forms of stewardship may arise from unexpected quarters? Of course we are talking here of something else than the questions of emergent nations and their part in the world community. But there is at least a parallel; and if the West has been shaped by Christianity, then there is more than a parallel. For the fruits of the gospel are what "stewardship" means; and by their fruits one can tell to whom the kingdom rightly belongs. Stewardship is not only a challenge to the West; it may very well be the test by which our faith is judged—and found wanting.

Land Use

Ritchie Calder, now professor of international relations at Edinburgh University, has written *Common Sense About a Starving World*.[8] In this little book he sketches the issues of production and consumption in the modern world, which he came to know as consultant to the specialized agencies of the United Nations. He suggests that the future of mankind will depend not only on the scientific fulfillment of Einstein's famous equation, $E = m c^2$, but on the less familiar but equally portentous formula, $C = B : E$. The latter means that the "carrying capacity" of the land ("C") depends on the balance between two other factors, the "biotic potential" or ability to produce plants, and the environmental resistance to this potential. The pressing problems of overpopulation and overproduction, for instance, are not meshed to help each other because we have not solved the other problem of distribution and its implications for political economy. In his chapter on "The Politics of Hunger," Calder describes the fate of the Food and Agricultural Organization, the first UN permanent agency, with John Boyd Orr as first Director-General.

At the Famine Conference in 1946 Orr's challenge to the nations was accepted, and famine was averted through self-denying ordinances (such as drastic rationing in Britain). But the further challenge to establish a World Food Board which would assist underdeveloped countries to increase production, and which would build up a reservoir of food and stabilize food prices—this was unacceptable: "Nations balked at the sacrifice of the fraction of sovereignty which it demanded." For one example, consider this statement: "The $4,000,000,000 which the U. S. Government has had to spend in buying farm produce to store and to rot, is far more than the whole world would have had to find in order to 'prime the pump' of a World Food Board and start that upward spiral which Boyd Orr prophesied." [9] Must we not confess that we in the West are rich not just *while* other nations are poor, but *because* they are poor? Until this fact—that our national economy is self-centered despite the claim of justice in behalf of the world community—enters into our stewardship, we are playing an ecclesiastical game. The church must challenge the nation with this radical nature of corporate stewardship. Certainly there is risk and sacrifice and controversy ahead for a nation which attempts such stewardship. But perhaps there is also the glory peculiar to the nation which responds.

This is but a beginning and outline of what needs to be said clearly and in detail by the church to the nation. So far the church has been so identified with the national economy that our stewardship simply confronted church members with the needs of the ecclesiastical organization for a share of their wealth. But now it is time to backtrack to the nature of property, to the way of earning our wealth and the price of our stewardship as measured in the hungry of our world. So we need to examine the nation and its stewardship, and our part within its life. We can-

not be proud of the part which Christians have played. We
have not been like leaven because we could not be told
apart from the whole, not by the way we earned and spent
our money at least. We said a lot and theorized, but now
we must begin to act in ways that will influence the nation
toward a reconciliation with other nations, and a service
to the needy. Thus will stewardship itself become the
proclamation of the gospel, the good news that in Jesus
Christ a new creation is present, a power to unite and to
forgive and to love. Thus will the nations learn what is
their glory and honor, the gift of Christ, King of kings and
Lord of lords, Healer of the nations.

NOTES FOR CHAPTER 7

1. Page 15 of Brock Chisholm's paper, "Freedom of Choice: the
   Ethics of Personal Responsibility," in *A Humane Society*, Rosen-
   berg, ed. (Toronto: University of Toronto Press, 1962).
2. The two phrases are from the WCC Division of Inter-Church
   Aid and Service to Refugees, Conference at Leysin, Switzer-
   land, on "Problems of International Migration and the Responsibility of the Churches." See report in *Christian Outlook*, Apr.,
   1964.
3. H. Richard Niebuhr, *Moral Man and Immoral Society* (New
   York: Charles Scribner's Sons, 1932), pp. 99f. See the entire
   Chapter 4, "The Morality of Nations."
4. The material in these paragraphs is taken from Joseph C. Mc-
   Lelland's "Dimensions of the Racial Crisis," in *Christian Outlook*, Nov., 1963.
5. See also Joseph C. McLelland, *The Other Six Days* (Richmond,
   Va.: John Knox Press, 1959), I.5, "The Gospel and Its Law."
6. *Cf.* Bruce Morgan, *Christians, the Church and Property* (Philadelphia: The Westminster Press, 1963), pp. 162ff: "The Trouble with Stewardship"; also the symposium in *Laity*, Nov., 1962:
   "Christians in Power Structures."
7. O. J. Lissitzyn, "International Law in a Divided World," *International Conciliation*, New York, March, 1963, p. 63. See
   also the volume *The Ethic of Power*, Harold J. Lasswell and
   Harlan Cleveland, eds. (New York: Harper & Row, Publishers,
   Inc., 1962), containing papers given at the Conference on Science, Philosophy and Religion, New York, 1960, especially

"World Ethic and World Revolution," by Harry B. Price, pp. 397ff.

8. (New York: The Macmillan Company, 1962).
9. Ritchie Calder, *op. cit.*

QUESTIONS FOR DISCUSSION

1. What should be done with North American farm surpluses? Technical know-how? The gospel of Jesus Christ?
2. Is the United States a Christian nation? In what sense or senses?
3. Does giving foods and services away overseas weaken the United States? Physically? Spiritually? Politically?
4. Is it wrong for the government to provide its citizens with Social Security which they could arrange on an individual basis?
5. Would it not be better to return to the nineteenth-century era of responsible individualism? Is individual responsibility more Christian than social responsibility?

Part III

THE ETHICS
OF
PROMOTION

---

by *James M. Gustafson*

Professor of Christian Ethics,
Yale Divinity School, Yale University,
New Haven, Connecticut

8

Stewardship

as Promotion

Institutional Success Versus Christian Witness

EVERY institution that continues to perpetuate itself and seeks to grow is involved in some kinds of promotion of itself. The acute dilemma for churches rests in our awareness that the proclaiming of God's deeds and God's will does not carry with it a guarantee of institutional success. One does not have to be a sectarian, or an adherent to exemplary sectarian ethics, to feel the force of the New Testament. There are many occasions in Christian history when obedience to God brought into question the institutional success of ecclesiastical organizations. There is no guarantee that faithfulness to Jesus Christ brings with it the recruitment of many new members to congregations and denominations. There is no assurance that obedience of God's will brings the earthly reward of increased giving to social organizations called churches. There is no law of automatic harmony which says that deep spiritual and moral commitment to God is coincident with institutional growth.

If we were representatives of a pure type of sectarian

witness to the gospel, the issues would be relatively clear. We could see that the churches are embedded in North American culture; that they have taken over procedures for the propagation of their message and life that are effective in other sectors of the economy and the society; that their bureaucracies grow with diversification of functions in the churches, and with the specialization of training and labor that is thus required. We could find the historical authority, and even a biblical authority, for rebellion in the ecclesiastical world; for secession from congregations given to rummage sales, and from denominations given to outright coercion of the clergy in order to bring in the money needed to run the denominational program.

Indeed, all of us are aware that the seeds of rebellion are already planted in the churches, and particularly in the commitments of young Christians. The voices that cry for a cultural disestablishment of the churches, that suggest that it is probably the vocation of some to be Christians outside of membership in churches, that tell us religion with its institutional demands gets in the way of obedient faith—these voices are being heard. And one would honestly have to suggest that they would not be heard if the churches had not themselves created the conditions of alienation and disaffection that cause some of the most morally sensitive Christians to follow these prophets.

Culture-Christianity

If we were representatives of a pure type of culture-Christianity that would identify what is good in the gospel with what is successful in the world, the issues would be relatively clear. We could say that true piety and institutional success were the warp and woof of God's saving presence in the world. We could feel secure in pointing to the growth of churches as a sign of the increase of faith, to the development of complex organizational structures with the wisdom of the serpents that is necessary for the propagation of the crucified Lord. We could say that the victorious reigning Christ is so in command of all things that he rules the patterns of our recruitment of church members and the ways in which we govern our ecclesiastical fiscal policies. We might even argue that an ethic of responsibility requires us to make compromises with the worldly ways around us in order to build parking lots that redound to the glory of God and to secure money by the manipulation of human needs for the sake of the vital moral and evangelical witness of the gospel.

Indeed, all of us are aware of the subtle temptations of culture-Christianity in a North American society that has not as yet found participation in church life incongruent with the scientific world view, technological progress, and the crises of nuclear war and social revolution. Probably we are also convinced that a rebellion against ecclesiastical institutions could last for one generation, and then would find itself making its own peace with the institutional world, establishing its own ways of recruiting members, retaining those of a birthright membership, and routinizing the procedures for the maintenance of "renewed" communities. Thus we find ourselves not quite at home in the social organizations of church life, and not quite alienated enough from them to leave.

If we belonged to legally established churches with state support and with vast invested church funds, another option could be given to us. We would not have to worry about the maintenance of the institution as much as we do, for church taxes and other funds would roll in with regularity to keep up the buildings, pay pastors' salaries, and keep the cemeteries neat. Custom might continue to dictate the propriety of the celebration of birth through the lovely rite of infant baptism, and the celebration of puberty through the rite of confirmation. Doctrine might come to our defense to say that in baptism children are actually baptized into Christ, who is really present in the sacrament, and that the purpose of the institution is to make known the continued objective presence of Christ through liturgy and preaching to those who are interested in sharing personally in what they already share through baptism. With this taken care of—legally, economically, through custom, and doctrinally—we could proceed in a highly creative fashion to establish the cells of true commitment among church members, and form the new institutions, the para-*Gemeinde* that are the location of the church militant. But this is no real option for North American churches, and, if it were, it is doubtful that many of us would take to it.

Voluntary Churches

This all points to the distinct social, ecclesiastical, and moral situation of North American Christians. We have voluntary churches, not in the sense that churches are like other voluntary associations in which humanly defined purposes draw like-minded people together to fulfill them, but in the sense that the continuation of an effective witness to the reality of God's presence is dependent upon the willing consent and participation of laity, giving their time and money and energy to the work of the institutional church. The democratic ethos, regardless of its historical origins, pervades the life of the churches in such a way that the laity often do conceive of them as analogous, in a simple way, to the other organizations to which they belong—that is, subject to the rule of the majority vote of the membership.

We are many denominated sectors of the whole Church in North America, and thus inevitably in competition with each other for the limited capital (money and persons)

that exists in the market, even though we are not trying
to drive each other out of business to set up a monopoly.
Morally, we have said, in effect, that the community is not
called to a pure, exemplary witness to the perfect obedience even to death—obedience to the way of suffering and
the way of the cross.

For theological reasons, as well as for reasons of cultural
convenience, we have assumed that the goodness of God is
made known in expensive temples of worship and centers
of activity. We have said that God's ways are not necessarily
antithetical to the ways of the world, and thus we can
borrow techniques for institutional perpetuation that have
been tried and tested in the nonreligious spheres of cultural life. We have said that the Christian community
is responsible for many of the human needs of men, and
thus we have routinized ways in which these can be met:
through day nurseries, through psychological counseling
services, through appeals for Church World Service,
through air-conditioned comfort while on our knees in
prayer. We have said that if the Christian community is
to accept responsibility for the genuine moral health of the
society, it must be in an established relationship to the
laity whose time and effort is spent welding the frames of
railroad cars or determining how the insurance premiums
are to be most beneficially invested or desegregating motels
and residential areas. We have said that an isolation from
the world would lead to irrelevance to the world, and we
would be willing to run the risks involved in a Christian
ethic that accepts responsibility for the morally ambiguous
state of human existence, even if this inevitably leads to
moral ambiguity in the conduct of the institutional life of
the Church.

This obviously places the church leader in an uncom-
fortable position. He might flee from it in search of a position that is less fraught with temptation, sin, and the wrath

of God; but it would be hard to find such a place in this world. He might identify himself with what it takes to run an effective institution in North America, and find the theological and moral reasons for doing this, but his own conscience might plague him when the radical critics call his behavior to his attention. He might engage in what Paul Ramsey has suggested, and which national leaders have to engage in when they think of the use of nuclear weapons—that is, "deferred repentance." The consequences of his actions would not be so far-reaching as those of the President of the United States, but he could put moral parentheses around his day-to-day activity and repent on Sunday; or, if he is busy promoting on Sunday too, he could repent when he retires. Or he might set up his situation in terms of the distance between the ideal and the actual, and work out a theory of compromise as the best solution to a nasty situation.

He might list the ideal ends, and the ideal means, and tell himself that he will divert from them only enough to achieve what is historically possible in Musselshell, Montana, or in Scarsdale, New York. He might find the rules for the conduct of the institution that would be least dissonant with a pure version of the gospel, and then find the reasons why exceptions could be made to these rules. The rule might say that the giving of the laity ought to come spontaneously from his gratitude for what God has done for man in Jesus Christ. The exception might be that it takes education to make men see what the rule is, and then the next exception might be that the line between education and manipulation is so thin that a little manipulation of the motivation is only slightly distorting to the symphony, such as one weak cellist in the cello section. After all, you cannot have a whole cello section of Pablo Casals.

The teacher of Christian ethics would be somewhat less

than responsible if he did not try to think about institutional ethics in the setting just delineated. Pastors and denominational executives exist in no less a complicated and ambiguous moral situation than do the laity. One does not need to be in politics or in finance to know the sharpness of moral decisions; one can be a leader in a congregation or in a denomination. If the author of this chapter has anything to contribute to the understanding of the ethics of church promotion, it is probably in confining his discussion henceforward to a limited language of ethics.

Language of Ethics and Church Promotion

A highly successful fund raiser for a private company that was widely used by churches a decade ago, on one occasion, reported to the writer the strategy of his success. His first principle was never to identify himself personally with either the situation of the pastor or the situation of the layman he was training. His point was this: if he felt with and for the pastor or the layman in terms of the stresses and strains they were under—moral or financial—he would mitigate his effectiveness in manipulating the total fund-raising drive. He would qualify his vision of the objective of the campaign (raising money) in such a way that his own usefulness would be limited.

His second principle was never to make the end for which the money was to be spent a primary object of appeal. His point was this: men are not persuaded to sacrificial giving by theological, ethical, or religious reasons. Rather, their giving comes from purely subjective attitudes, desires, and impulses.

His third principle was to find and use the symbols, words, and deeds that most persuasively unleash the need to give, regardless of any ethical or theological convictions that might bring these procedures under judgment. If status-competition is what it takes, use it; if Bible quoting is what it takes, use it. As an entrepreneur who had in effect prostituted his theological education and ordination, perhaps he was working within a different set of moral expectations from persons who are engaged by churches and denominations, but obviously churches raised no serious questions about this prostitution. Thus, this seems to be a fair but extreme example to which we might turn our attention. At this point we are concerned not so much to make moral judgments on this promotional procedure as to illustrate the ways in which we can get at the moral questions.

His own ethic of church promotion is fairly clear. There is an end: the raising of a stipulated amount of money for a local congregation. The end beyond that end—what the money was to be used for—was incidental to his work. Given the end, those means were morally viable that most efficiently and successfully fulfilled the end. Neither end nor means were then brought under any other criteria of moral judgment.

Ends and Means

One might use the same formal end-means schematism and come out with a different procedure; this we must note. One might say that the end to be served is the glorification of God and the propagation of his ways and will among men. Some conviction about the importance of these ends would be required if an appeal on the basis of them was to evoke sacrificial giving from the members of the congregation. Somehow the remoteness of God in the minds of the people would have to be overcome; that requires a rather substantial job of evangelization and education. A sophisticated interpretation of how the raising of X thousand dollars and the construction of a new unit glorifies God and makes his ways known would have

to be made. And certainly the *means* by which the sub-
sidiary end of a financial success would be achieved would
have to be consonant with the glorification of God. One
could hardly glorify God through the use of means that
are abrasive to his known ways. Simply put, the ultimate
purpose would inform and judge the means used to its
achievement.

If one is morally distressed by the rather unscrupulous
way in which our fund-raising informer dealt with things,
one might be prompted to develop a set of rules to avoid
overstepping the bounds of moral propriety: (1) one
might stipulate that the promoter ought always to identify
himself with the persons he is seeking to influence, for
such personal relationships are an expression of the "being-
for-others" and "being-with-others" that is the life of Christian love; (2) the purposes for which money is being
raised ought to have theological and moral justification,
for without this there is no rational basis for judging
whether they belong within the framework of Christian
community life; (3) those who are asked to support a
church promotional enterprise ought to be convinced of
its objective religious validity; (4) human beings are to
be treated as ends in themselves, and not merely as technical means; (5) motivation for giving ought to be
prompted by and governed by convictions about the importance of the Christian faith, and appeals that subvert
this are to be ruled out of bounds. These five rules might
be used to avoid what is morally culpable about the procedure of the professional fund raiser.

The question for the church promoter, then, is this: How
does one use rules of conduct? Are they to be judged
eternally valid and immutable, and then to be prescrip-
tively applied to particular situations? Do they present
the *outside limits,* the line beyond which one will not go?
Or are they to be seen as *illuminating,* as "lights" that in-

dicate what the pitfalls of a certain course of action will be, and in what direction our action ought to go? Americans, we know, are much given to the development of ethical codes for various professions, occupations, and activities. If there is moral scandal, the American impulse is to form a new code that will prohibit it from occurring again. The question of the use of codes or rules is profoundly important.

Moral Rules

One can turn to H. Richard Niebuhr's *The Responsible Self* [1] for one indication of the basic model of human action that is involved if rules are taken to be extrinsic norms that have a kind of legal validity. He suggests you will find man the citizen, the rule-obeying creature. The right action is then determined by his conformity to objective and extrinsic moral propositions. If driven to an extreme, then morality is reduced to the question of obedience to propositions, rather than to any creative activity and response. One can see, then, that code-determined conduct can violate something of the basic moral nature of the church promoter, as it can every other man.

If moral rules, however, do not have a kind of legal authority, they can still have importance in showing the way in which men ought to go. But action is not simply application of one or two rules; action is determined as the next steps in a promotional campaign in a particular congregation or denomination are illuminated by a number of moral propositions, which may not be totally consistent with each other in the abstract. For example, we ought not to treat the laity as if they were the technical means for our use to promote an institutional end. If this was the exclusive "rule," we could spend more time than it is worth deciding at which particular point an "end in itself" becomes a means to another end. We would be arguing about the occasions when it is legitimate to make exceptions to the rule. Ecclesiastical moral life is more dynamic, faster moving than rules are, and if this is the sole procedure we use, perhaps we are limited unduly in our work.

Responsibility

There is yet another model of ethical interpretation that can be used in the analysis of church promotion. It is a "responsibility" model. This one comes at us in this decade from a great variety of sources: Father Bernhard Häring uses it in his massive moral theology textbook, *The Law of Christ* [2]; H. Richard Niebuhr uses it in his way in *The Responsible Self;* philosophers are also exploring its importance. The writer of this chapter would use it by asking some basic questions: To whom is the church promoter responsible? For what is he responsible? To whom was the fund raiser in the preceding example responsible? To his organization. For what? For the success of a campaign within the purposes stipulated by his employing firm.

In the author's brief experience as a pastor in the early 1950's, these became guiding questions. When his denomination was running a building loan fund campaign, he received a letter from the regional director saying that as a young pastor who might be seeking a larger church, it would be important for him to set a good record in regard to fund raising, and thus to have the Northford Congregational Church accept its apportioned request for the campaign. To whom was he responsible? The executive? Or God? Was his future success in the escalator of church prestige that for which he was responsible to God? Or, if he sought to govern his activities in the light of the knowledge of God who called him to his ministry, did he define that for which he was responsible differently? And if the Northford church was to accept its apportioned goal, was it to be persuaded on the grounds of its responsibility for his professional success, or on the grounds of the ways in which a building loan fund could be an instrument for the pursuit of theologically viable purposes of the church?

The situation of the church promoter is without doubt not an easy one within a "responsibility" model of interpretation. As we noted early in the chapter, there is no guarantee that obedience to God guarantees institutional success. The pastor works in the voluntary church, where his leadership is always "political." Yet every committed Christian leader would wish to confess he is responsible to God for the furthering of the activities which are in accord with the purposes of God—activities of evangelization, pastoral care, education, moral action, and worship. He is also responsible to the denomination, the congregation, the institution in various of its social organizations. His choice in the extreme is to bracket God out for practical purposes, and to operate as if he alone were responsible for institutional promotion. Or his choice is to reflect upon the purposes for which he is responsible to God, and then on the institutional procedures that are effective in achieving some of those purposes. But his work is not merely a means-ends scheme. The pastor is responsible to God for the procedures used to fulfill the purposes. Are they part of a manner of life that is worthy of the gospel?

As an undergraduate this writer made a study of the Youth for Christ movement for a social psychology course, and in the process attended some Saturday night rallies at Chicago's Orchestra Hall. After one of them, he visited the men's room, and observed a zealous "personal worker" taking advantage of the time men spent in that room to engage in his evangelical activity! Is such practical exercise of evangelical zeal worthy of the gospel?

Not only are church promoters responsible to God for the determination of the purposes of their activity and for the procedures used to fulfill the purposes, but they bear responsibility for the consequences of their activity. In church promotion it would seem that we might have too limited a view of consequences. We seek one end, the achievement of which we feel to be the consequence of the promotion—the raising of X thousand dollars. But there are also the consequences of the way in which that money is raised—and here we refer more to the effects on the good will of the people. The way in which things are done evokes responses in the laity inside and outside the church. That response is probably in the form of a judgment (well or ill-informed) about *what is witnessed to in church promotion.* Actions of church promotion are exemplary in the sense that they witness to the fundamental functioning morality and beliefs of church leadership. If they witness to an institution-centered notion of responsibility, they will evoke a response that the churches are merely self-perpetuating institutions.

The conduct of church promotion, then, ought to express the community's sense of responsibility to God's will and work; the purposes of church promotion ought to be governed similarly by theological convictions. The instruments and techniques can never be so abrasive to the gospel that they smog the witness of the church to Jesus Christ.

Notes for Chapter 8

1. H. Richard Niebuhr, *The Responsible Self* (New York: Harper & Row, Publishers, Inc., 1963).
2. Father Bernhard Häring, *The Law of Christ* (Westminster, Md.: Newman Press, Vol. I, 1961; Vol. II, 1963).

QUESTIONS FOR DISCUSSION

1. Can advertising "sell" Christian faith?
2. Should people stay out of membership in the church for the *right* reasons? What are some?
3. Do people sometimes join the church for the wrong reasons?
4. What are the proper conditions for membership in the Church of Jesus Christ?
5. Is "success" in church membership and finance a work of God? Or of the devil?
6. Was there a connection between Jesus' driving the money changers from the Temple and his crucifixion a few days later?
7. Who are the modern "money changers" in the Temple?
8. Is it proper for a church to employ "outsiders" (professional campaigners) to raise money for building purposes? Architects? Lawyers? Pastors?

9

Evangelism as Promotion

Ethics of Intentions and Objective Ethics:
The Problems of Subjective and Objective Appeals

IN an essay, *"Grundprobleme der Ethik,"* published first in 1902, Ernst Troeltsch raises the issue whether Christian ethics deals primarily with the intentions and motives of men for action, or whether it provides some objective criteria for the determination of the goals, the states of affairs that are to be the consequences of actions. When we are thinking about the relation of the Christian faith to human action, are we to attend primarily to the ways in which the faith alters, transforms, and renews certain dispositions, motives, and intentions? Or are we to attend to some bases by which the Christian revelation gives objective criteria for judging what ought to take place in the world? To put the alternatives yet another way, does the gospel engender a motive and an intention—to love, to do the loving things? Or does the gospel provide norms by which we judge what act more or less realizes the norm of love in human affairs, the principles of God's reign in the social order?

The issue may appear on first glance to be one for professors to write about in books read only by other professors. We are convinced, however, that ecclesiastical institutions are subtly involved in choices on this basic issue in their promotional efforts, and that further exploration of the issues might shed light on the moral questions of institutional church life.

There are two levels at which the issue can be turned on our concern for church promotion. The first can be indicated by these questions: Do we conduct evangelism and stewardship work as if the motivation, the intention, is the important thing to be affected? Or do we conduct evangelism and stewardship work as if there were objective criteria related to theological convictions that judge whether the patterns of visible human activity are the important things to be affected? Do we appeal primarily to motives, or do we appeal primarily to ends? What is the operating ecclesiastical ethic that is made concrete in our literature and in our activities?

Is This Evangelism?

The *New York Times* of Friday, July 3, 1964, carried an article about Stan Freberg, the comedian, as an evangelist, providing up-to-date means for calling men back to God and the Church through jazzy spot commercials on the radio:

The commercials . . . were recorded by a chorus and a 30-piece orchestra. They have a modern, unmistakably jazzy beat. "Doesn't it get a little lonely out on that limb, without Him?" the chorus sings. "Why try to go it alone? The blessings you lose may be your own!" Another one is described as follows: Before the music begins, the voice of someone, obviously a nonchurchgoer, explains: "We'll trot along one of these Sundays. Two weeks? The whole world could blow up by then." A deadpan voice replies, "That's right." [1]

A parenthetical observation is the first to be made. These announcements are endorsed by a denomination that is not noted for coddling the appeals of the latter-day New Thought enthusiasts such as Mr. Peale. Indeed, this denomination has been the source of many of the criticisms of the religious appeal to psychological needs that represents the by now well-flagellated Pealism. Nor is this denomination noted for its sponsorship of the more traditional and dramatic appeals to human fears that sometimes flood the world through loudspeakers in front of Billy Graham, and less respectable hawkers of Christianity. It is mainline, "theologically revived," "morally renewed" Protestantism that produces these "spots." The old gospel chorus, "And he walks with me and he talks with me," would hardly disgrace the decorum of a liturgically self-conscious worship service in 90 per cent of the local congregations of the sponsoring church.

Yet what is the center of the appeal? Loneliness on the limb without Him. The appeal obviously is to a psychic need that is magnified in its proportions by existence in depersonalized urban American cities. What is the promise if you have Him on the limb with you? "Why try to go it alone? The blessings you lose may be your own!" We submit that the promise, insofar as it is clear at all—and it reeks with ambiguity—is for the benefits of emotional security that might accrue from Him. The appeal itself is to subjective states in persons, and the reasons for finding Him are the subjective satisfactions that will be forthcoming by not going it alone. Who is the "Him"? Supposedly it is whoever the listener wants to make Him. It is the grandfatherly God who holds our hand as we get farther and farther out on the limb (it is probably a broad limb, if there is room for two). He squeezes our hand a bit when threats come, so we feel stronger in the face of our loneliness. It is one portrait or another of Jesus, the one that most readily fits the feeling that is evoked by the commercial; probably it is the Sunday School book illustration of

Jesus the shepherd surrounded by lambs and children, saying in King James English, "Suffer the little children to come unto me."

The appeal is supposed to be evangelical and promotional. And since it is directed to a widespread emotional need on the part of modern man, it is probably sited on the target of getting a bigger share of the loneliness market for Him, rather than for alcohol, "cheesecake," psychiatrists, or the fellowship of the beat. The object of appeal is a disposition, and if there is a moral justification for the conduct of the appeal in these terms, it is obviously to the intention of the religious huckster. Modern man intends to do good (perhaps for lonely people rather than for God), but the message that expresses his intention has been brought under very flimsy objective criteria for judgment drawn from Christian convictions about who the "Him" is, or from ethics pertaining to whether one is being responsible to God and to the tradition of the faith by making this appeal both in its substance and in its form.

We all know that one may become more lonely rather than less lonely by committing oneself to Jesus Christ; that the limb may be longer, thinner, and more treacherous, and that (if the author may also huckster a bit) it might lead to two limbs shaped into a cross. "The blessings you lose may be your own," we are told. True, there are appeals to beatitude and to health and to eternal life in the Scriptures, but the grounds upon which these gifts of God will be given are hardly made clear by the Stan Freberg-produced religious commercial. In the Bible they are God's blessings, and not our own, and the blessings of God are hardly to be thought of solely in terms of absence of anxiety or absence of loneliness.

"We'll trot along one of these Sundays. Two weeks? The whole world could blow up by then." "That's right," says the deadpan voice. Now if Oral Roberts screamed that the

world might come to an end in two weeks and thus you
had better get right with God, we would say that this appeal to fear is reprehensible in the light of both doctrine
and ethics. Does the jazzy beat transform the message?
Or does it merely give it a new package? Is the church
bringing its evangelical activities under any objective theological and ethical criteria when it looks with disdain
upon others who package the same half-truths in older
wineskins, and then peddle them in new attractive bottles?
A minister commented to the press that the punch lines
"leave them with something to think about." True, but so
does the illustrated moral philosophy of *Playboy*. So does
Mr. Clean. What is it the churches want men to think
about? About the possibility that the world may blow up
in two weeks? About getting to church next Sunday rather
than two weeks from now, just in case the blow-up comes?

The author is reminded of the last sermon he heard in
an Army chapel at an embarkation area during World War
II, just before the men boarded a troopship to cross the
Pacific. Two sizes of cable and rope, and one piece of
string, were draped from the front of the pulpit. The troops
were given "something to think about" when the clinching
line of the preacher was, "If a Japanese submarine sinks
your ship, will your lifeline to heaven be this—or this—
or (lifting the string) this?" That was something to think
about. Now the consolation of a word of God's love and
providence is not to be scoffed at in a moment of deep
dread; but were they to think about the goodness and
power of God as testified in the victory of Christ? Or were
they to think about themselves—their lifeline to heaven?
To think about the goodness and power of God is also sub-
jectively meaningful and satisfying, but something persua-
sive has to be said about the object of faith to which we
are called before the consolation comes.

Why go to church before the world blows up in two

weeks? It doesn't say. Maybe the preacher performs magical rites there that protect one. Maybe he has powerful tranquilizers. It may be also that the preacher should call the wrath of God down upon a people who let the world get into a state where men could blow it up in two weeks. But one would go home more shaken than when he came.

Motives

The Stan Freberg evangelistic commercials reflect an operational ethic and a functioning pattern of activity on the part of the church. We are working on the emotions, the fears, the loneliness, the anxieties of men. The commercials set up a vague pattern of promises or threats that evoke a mood. The mood is being evoked for what end? That is left vague. The intention of the manipulator of someone else's subjective state is not made specific in his actions. Loneliness on the limb might be alleviated as much by a good healthy friendship as by vague references to "Him." It might temporarily be relieved by a pleasant time in bed with a "Her." There is content to the word God that is full, rich, relatively unambiguous, threatening as well as consoling, judging as well as redeeming. This is left out. We are not merely subjective beings affecting other persons' subjectivity. There is, rather, validity to the knowledge of God that is given in Christian faith. We are responsible to God, to lead men to the acknowledgment of God as their Lord. We are something less than responsible to him for others when we focus on the evoking of feelings without bringing both the ends we have in view for this activity, and the way in which we engage in it, into accord with the Christian knowledge of God.

To be sure, to evoke any response is to appeal to a person's affections, his desires, his feelings, his subjectivity. Men do not come to faith by rational argumentation, this we know. But the appeal to the affections is for the sake of God. If we do not make clear that God, in the face of Jesus Christ, is the one to whom men are to respond, we are simply moving them for other purposes: to get them to church (confusing evangelism with a recruitment job) or to bring them psychic satisfactions. The procedures by which an appeal is made cannot be dissonant with the purpose for which they are made.

The Problem of Judgment by Intention or by Objective Criteria

The first level to which the polarization of subjective-dispositional approach and objective-criterial approach could be turned was the actual practice of church promotion. The second is the level of judging ourselves as responsible church leaders. What are our principles of self-criticism in church promotion? Our subjectivity? The rectitude of our attitudes, dispositions and intentions? Or some objective criteria derived from Scripture and theology about the ends toward which our work is directed? In the area of political ethics, we are aware of the significance of the differentiation involved. Reinhold Niebuhr's critique of the Christian ethics of subjective intention has made a fruitful mark on North American Protestant thinking: men can do evil from good motives. What is needed is an objective ethic by which what they actually do can be judged and guided by norms derived from the gospel. This issue as it applies to church promotion was dealt with in part in the previous chapter.

Christian ethics is unmistakably an ethics of disposition in some of its dimensions. We are to be loving; the motive is very important. We are to be free from bondage to traditional ways of self-justification, including legalism. But it is not totally dispositional. Paul tells us, "All things are lawful, but not all things are helpful." "All things are lawful, but not all things build up." The first side of each statement can be taken to point to the inner disposition of freedom in the Christian; the second side points to the need for some reflection about what the proper expression of the disposition is to be.

The church promoter might well turn to the proclamation of Christian freedom for his license to love God and do what he pleases, to avoid excessive scrupulosity in the development of promotional techniques. Or he can point to the autonomy of the technical world, which in effect tells him: "If you live in North America in the 1960's, there are certain ways by which things get done, whether you are launching a political campaign, a new labor union, or a church building fund. The ways of the world are with us: there is no point in trying to avoid them, or trying to work differently."

Is This Christian Love?

A young conscientious Christian banker in the Southwest narrated for the writer an occasion in his early business career about which he had some moral unrest. At the age of 28 he was vice-president in charge of new business for a large and growing bank. He was asked by the local Salvation Army officer to head up the local campaign for funds. He agreed to do it after considering the invitation in the light of three considerations: (1) it would be good for new business for the bank if it was known in the city that this able young executive was willing to take on this particular social responsibility; (2) it would be good for his own future in the bank if the senior executives saw he was willing to take on such a project; (3) it would be good for the Salvation Army since he had confidence in his fund-raising ability. His procedure in forming his committee was as follows: First, he went to three other successful young executives, about his own age, his own level of responsibility in business, his own income level, belonging to churches like the one he belonged to and to the same prestige level of clubs in the city. From these men he got promises that they would seriously consider working with him in the project, but he did not work for a commitment from any of them on the first round. Then he went to a man of the same age with a more prominent business position, with more income, with higher social prestige, and worked on him until he acquiesced and committed himself. He returned then to the other three, and "they fell like dominoes." The result was the "best damned Salvation Army fund campaign in the history of the city."

Certainly this man's statement of intentions, and surely his procedures, are not totally foreign to promoters of religious institutions. Perhaps one difference is that he knew what he was doing and thus could plan things that way, whereas sometimes church leaders are not so self-conscious about what they are up to, or cover it over with piety. Was he right or was he wrong? If we run this story through an ethical analysis, we can first look at his intentions. They were unambiguously self-centered, though he did see that his acceptance of social responsibility would promote his own welfare. They were not merely bank centered, though he found a happy coincidence between his altruism and what was good for the bank. They were also moved by what would be good for the Salvation Army, a worthy organization. Let us hypothetically put ourselves in the man's place. Would we judge our motives and say that our intentions were on the whole good, even though the interest to be promoted was partly that of self and partly that of the economic institution in which we worked? Was the happy coincidence of mutual benefit to the executive, to the bank, and to human service real? Or was self-interest, or bank-interest, the first source of motivation, and the desire to serve the downtrodden and oppressed merely a good reason to further other ends? We might say that motivation is too complex to judge, and too slippery to pin down.

Or would we say that the judgment about proper motivation cannot be taken out of context? We also have to look at the procedures used and the consequences that occurred. We probably would say that the procedures were clearly manipulative—self-consciously so. The banker used a higher status man to recruit those who aspired to the same status. How do we judge this procedure? By the intention of its author? This is already ambiguous, for he intended three things, each of which seemed to enhance the other. Or are there objective ethical norms that say that no matter how good the intentions, this self-conscious manipulation of persons is morally wrong? It uses men as technical means. In the name of one man's mixed but higher motives, he appeals to the status motivation of other men. Is there discord between this kind of status-manipulation and how men are called upon to relate to each other as they witness to the God of freedom and of love? If there is an objective ethic, related to the gospel, that makes us uneasy about this means of procedure, do we abandon it? Revise it? Compromise it? Or do we say that the end to be sought, namely more money for public service in the city, gives moral justification to the procedures?

Moral Judgments

If we decide that the Christian ethical approach to promotion is to be related primarily to our intentions, and our intentions are reasonably good (they stem from a motive to seek the good of many neighbors, and seek the ends that will serve the good), then perhaps we need not worry so much about procedures. If, however, we say that there

are some indications in the Christian faith and life that
persons are to be treated in certain ways, and that we
violate their integrity and autonomy if we treat them in
other ways, the question of the procedures is open indeed.
Does this particular procedure witness to the gospel? The
use that will be made of the money will. The intention of
the leader is at least partly to seek the good of others. But
is the procedure consonant with Christian belief? We
could argue that procedures are technical and thus amoral.
Thus the use of nuclear weapons is amoral; it is the intention of the user (and the effects of winning a war) that is
the moral question. The manipulation of persons is technical and amoral, it might be said. But to say this, is not to
bring the procedures also under the judgment of the gospel, which has an objective importance.

If church leaders focus the questions of moral judgment
primarily on their intentions, they apparently have more
freedom to decide what procedures will fulfill the intentions. They intend to be evangelical, so the practices of
evangelism can be crude, bubbleheaded, and manipulative. They intend to raise money for a cause that is generally worthy, and thus whatever coaxes money out of
people is worthy of use.

If church leaders focus the questions of moral judgment
on the concrete ends to be achieved, and if these ends are
theologically viable, they run the risk of being less persua-
sive, and thus less effective. To proclaim God's faithfulness
to men, and the command of man's faithfulness to God—
so starkly and realistically made known in Jesus Christ—
will probably bring fewer people to church.

If church leaders focus the questions of moral judgment
primarily on the procedures to be used in church promotion, they will feel restricted in the techniques that can be
fittingly used for the sake of the gospel. If the techniques
are to be governed by the Christian faith, if they also wit-

ness to our responsibility to God, the institutional success of the ecclesiastical venture might be more subdued.

In spite of the difficulties involved, ecclesiastical leadership needs to bring ethical considerations to bear upon each point of its policy making and activity. Given the moral, ecclesiastical, and social situation of voluntary churches in North America, there is no easy and pure way in which institutional success and moral responsibility to God walk hand in hand on pleasant paths through a garden of roses in the cool of the evening. Yet ecclesiastical leadership cannot be paralyzed by its complicated moral situation. Institutionalized Christianity is a necessity; the continuation of the Christian witness to God in history requires human institutions that are effective instruments of God's presence, God's way, and God's will.

The professor of Christian ethics cannot come in with a book of rules, or a means-ends pattern that church leaders adopt as an extrinsic authoritative moral code to be followed legalistically. If he tried this, he would be assuming too much upon himself, for his responsibilities are never quite that of institutional leaders. He would also be seeking to relieve the leaders from serious moral reflection on their own activities. What the professor can do is limited, namely help the responsible leader to see what moral questions need to be brought self-consciously into the reflection and action of the church, to show some of the ways in which church promoters might reflect upon their duties in terms of ethics. The time and place of the morally responsible decisions are occasions of witness to God, or obedience and disobedience to God.

Church promotion is a moral activity in which leaders are immediately involved. In its basic forms, in its required patterns of reflection, in its difficulties for decisions, in its ambiguity and complexity, it is not really different from other areas of moral action. In the intensity of its sense of obligation and conscientiousness to God, perhaps it is different. For the institution witnesses to the faith in its practice in a highly visible and audible way.

NOTE FOR CHAPTER 9

1. © 1964 by The New York Times Company. Reprinted by permission.

QUESTION FOR DISCUSSION

1. Should the church set up high ethical standards for its members, even though this may result in fewer members?

Part IV

THE
DENOMINATIONAL
STRUCTURE

---

by *Spencer P. Austin*

Executive Secretary of Unified Promotion, Disciples of Christ, Indianapolis, Indiana

10

The Denominational Structure

as Christ's Instrument

IT is somewhat anomalous that a member of the Disciples of Christ in a promotional workshop should have been assigned to present the subject, "The Denominational Structure as Christ's Instrument." This communion historically has resisted being called a denomination and has never developed a universally accepted apologetic for the existence—let alone the support—of agencies and instrumentalities of the Church. Indeed this communion came into being as a protest movement against the ecclesiolatry of the excessive denominationalism of the eighteenth and nineteenth centuries.

Be that as it may, this was a pertinent assignment in the context of such a gathering. After discussing together the New Testament motives for giving, the ethics of promotion, the materials and media of communication, and the meaning of corporate stewardship, it would be most ironic if we should suddenly discover that the Church itself and the denominational structures within which all of us work were completely irrelevant to the mission of Christ and were thereby invalid and unworthy of support.

If we should go even further and find them incapable of being made relevant, it would be catastrophic.

Attacks on Church Structure

This is a day when the accent on structured religion is frequently called into question. Many of the questions apply to all structures of the Church and not just those of a denominational nature. These questions are so much the "atmosphere" in a number of American seminaries and in the Church as a whole that there is considerable avoidance of the pastoral ministry as a vocation even among theological students.

The current mood of cynicism regarding the church, especially at the local level, is popularized in the little book, *Where in the World?* written by Colin W. Williams.[1] It is Mr. Williams' thesis that the church as we know it today is a hopelessly outmoded structure, incapable of performing its primary mission.

Another volume, more helpfully written, is that of Daniel Jenkins entitled *Beyond Religion.* Jenkins reminds us that there are interesting notions afloat which

. . . express the belief that mature Christian faith can exist independently of the religious activities with which it has always been closely associated and that . . . this is the only form in which it can exist for many people today. Discussion of them started as a result of some brief observations made along these lines by Dietrich Bonhoeffer, in letters written from prison.[2]

In reviewing the receptivity to these notions, Jenkins points out that many of those most interested in a "religionless Christianity" (that is, a nonstructured and therefore nonchurch-related and noninstitutionally expressed faith) include those

... who would be considered by ordinary standards to be notably "religious" Christians, professional theologians and exceptionally well-informed lay leaders of the churches. What is more, among these they have often been those who have been most vocal in asserting the uniqueness and distinctiveness of the revelation of God in Christ, as recorded in Scripture and as proclaimed by the Church.[3]

In 1961 Eberhard Bethge sought to identify four limiting characteristics of religion in terms of Bonhoeffer's outlook. He listed them as follows: (1) individualistic preoccupation with one's own self and interior states; (2) metaphysical, with God brought in to complete as the supernatural a fundamentally man-centered view of reality; (3) interest in one department of life primarily and that tending to be pushed into insignificance by scientific discovery; and (4) the God of religion as a *deus ex machina,* one who comes onto the stage from the outside to help his children when they are in trouble, rather than a being who is at the very core of existence.

Bonhoeffer

This critique on the trappings of religion, including both its practices and structures, is not directed exclusively toward any particular denomination, nor toward denominationalism *per se,* but toward an undue emphasis on religion, or religiosity, in contrast to primary Christian faith. It strikes at the institutionalism and preoccupation with the formalities of religion seen in all denominations. Two citations from Bonhoeffer's writings, edited by Bethge in *Prisoner for God,* will illustrate the point of view:

The religious act is always something partial, faith is always something whole, an act involving the whole of life. Jesus does not call men to a new religion, but to life.[4]

And again:

One must abandon every attempt to make something of oneself, whether it be a saint, a converted sinner, a churchman [the priestly type so-called!], a righteous man or an unrighteous one, a sick man or a healthy one. This is what I mean by worldliness [called by the Bonhoeffer cult holy worldliness]—taking life in one's stride, with all its duties and problems, its successes and failures, its experiences and helplessness. It is in such a life that we throw ourselves utterly in the arms of God and participate in His sufferings in the world and watch with Christ in Gethsemane. That is faith, that is metanoia, and that is what makes a man Christian.[5]

There is a wholesome challenge in these brief passages to give primacy to faith in God through Christ. This is entirely as it should be. It is a perversion of this challenge, however, to overlook the fact that the Church itself was called into being by Christ precisely for the purpose of keeping alive the challenge to primary obedience and to make possible recurrent renewal among those who tend to fall by the wayside.

Bonhoeffer, however, should not be given too much of the credit for the current criticisms which are being heaped upon religious structure and practice. The rediscovery of Kierkegaard has also played its part, and we should not overlook the influence of Karl Barth in this area, especially his *Church Dogmatics* [6] and the chapter entitled "The Revelation of God as the Abolition of Religion." Nor should we fail to note that much of the biblical theology of our day has brought into focus for the modern church the realization that Jesus himself was often in conflict with religion and the structural barriers it had erected to the divine-human fellowship.

Jenkins properly reminds us:

It is only when the Church recognizes that faith lies beyond religion, as a gift from the Godward side to man, which judges

the religion of the Church as well as that of other communities
and which can find expression only in self-forgetting love,
that it is in a position to use the only resources provided for it
by its Lord to prevent it from becoming conformed like any
other institution to this world which passes away. Where this
recognition is not made, the Church may rapidly become an
impressive institution—indeed it may find it all the easier to do
so—but it will no longer be the servant of the Divine purpose.
Its very religiousness will do no more than confirm and celebrate its secularization.[7]

If time permitted, we might discuss the one significant
example of nonstructured religion, the *Mukyokai* (mu-
kyo-kai) *shugi,* or "no-church" movement of Japan which
has a wide fellowship in that country and which is of considerable interest in this. This is a movement without
clergy, ordinances, or organization of any kind. Indeed,
it decries organization of any sort. It is solely dependent
upon *sensai,* "teachers," with charismatic leadership. It is a
deliberate effort to promulgate the Christian faith without becoming a religion.

In the midst of this post-World War II theological fer-
ment, which has challenged the mores, the practices, and
the loyalties to structured religion in contrast to a basic
loyalty to God, four other factors have converged since to
develop a more formidable challenge to denominationalism
as such. These are the mobility of population, the emphasis
on the ecumenical Church, the will toward Christian
unity, and the widespread preoccupation with restructure.

The mobility of population has acquainted Christians
with congregational practices and emphases across denominational lines. This has tended to break down many
barriers which had long stood from lack of knowledge.
The emphasis on the ecumenical Church and the growing
will toward Christian unity have combined to produce a
widespread uneasiness at calling any denomination a

"Church." Furthermore, the emphasis upon restructure, which has been taking place throughout most of the denominations, has tended to bring into focus the ambiguous relation of denominations to the Church universal.

These factors are so self-evident that it does not seem necessary to provide supporting documentation. Suffice it to say that the milieu of theological, sociological, and denominational changes of the last twenty years has been conducive neither to the development of abiding denominational loyalties, locally or nationally, nor to the enlistment of enthusiastic financial support.

The Role of Denominational Structure

Let us now turn to a consideration of denominational structures and their functions "as Church" in the contemporary American scene. Biblically speaking, the term "church" may be properly applied generally to a local congregation, to the Church universal or to all Christians living within a particular geographical locality. Strictly speaking, therefore, a denomination is not and cannot be THE church, or even A church in the New Testament sense. At best it is only a manifestation of Church. Nevertheless, in the divine-human encounter of its existence, it must respond to the utmost as if it were THE church, the ecclesia, the "called-out" of God. It must embody within itself, to the best of its ability, the purposes, obligations, and attributes of the Christ.

The ambiguity of the situation stems partly from our history and reflects the divergent streams of ethnic origins which have populated the North American continent. It also stems partly from our imperfect understanding of the divine will and our imperfect appropriation of the divine Spirit. The paradox of our situation is that the more nearly we become THE church, the more sensitive we shall become to our brethren of other denominations and backgrounds, and the more readily we shall join with them in the service of the Master.

Denominational divisions impose limitations upon the body of Christ which are very real. Each denomination must be equally sensitive to the relationships which must be maintained with all other Christians as well as to the primary obligation to its role of servanthood in the world. The divisions between denominations are basically wrong, but the structures by which each seeks to implement the will of God to the best of its understanding may truly be instruments in the hands of Christ. The determining factor is whether or not these instruments are "in His hands."

Nels Ferré in his extended parable, *The Sun and the Umbrella*, points out in his chapter dealing with "the Church as Umbrella" that the Church is constantly subjected to pressures, strains, and conflicts which tempt it to become legalistic, sectarian, and authoritarian to the point of defending and promoting its structures and institutions rather than its Lord.

On the other hand, says Ferré:

Whenever the Church will learn to trust the power of the Holy Spirit to direct its life, whenever the Church will learn that He is a personal agent present in history, whenever the Church will appropriate the truth that it is rooted and grounded in God only when it is itself constituted basically by the personal presence of the Spirit—then, and only then, will the Church escape being an Umbrella and become evangelical according to its own true nature. Then it will neither dare nor need to domesticate the Holy Spirit and usurp His place by its organization. *Then* the institution will stand both under present judgment and present radical renewal. *Then* the Church will change with as much flexibility as the creative newness of human need, while being held steady by the faithfulness of God.[8]

We shall not attempt to discuss at this point the questions of ecclesiastical authority or varied ecclesiastical form. If one is interested in a review of the question of authority especially, and the basically divergent points of view of Liberal and Neo-Orthodox theologians, James Luther Adams' chapter in *Religion and Culture* [9] will be found helpful. This chapter is a treatment of Rudolph Sohm's theology of law and spirit, his equation of any dependence upon divine church law as "an expression of original sin," and a discussion of alternate points of view.

The Early Church

Our purpose is to deal with the function of structure rather than its authority or possible form. In this connection it is instructive to see its development in the early Church. The same justification one would give for establishing structures in the New Testament period is justification today if the denomination is seriously intent upon playing the role for which the Church was called into being.

Structure in the first-century Church came about in response to need. God's love had been made manifest in the Suffering Servant who called men to follow him in a fellowship of servanthood. His followers were to proclaim in word and deed God's yearning love for every human being throughout the inhabited earth. To that end their mission was one of service and proclamation.

Structures developed in the fulfillment of this mission. Structure was a tool for the extension of the faith, a means of preserving the purity of the Church, a requirement for the processes of spiritual renewal.

Structure was always treated as a means to an end, never as an end in itself. The focal point of emphasis was always the mission to be fulfilled or the need to be met. Structure was instrumental in achieving the divine purpose, but it was never to be confused with being the divine purpose.

Examples of the development of structure in the early Church make this point clear. The apostolate constituted the early leadership in the Church stemming directly from personal association with Jesus. Later a relief and welfare committee was appointed in the Jerusalem congregation to meet the problems of the hungry Grecian widows whose neglect had become a negation of the proclamation of the Church (Acts 6). At this point in its development added structure was necessary to preserve both the unity and the integrity of the Church.

The apostles and elders at Jerusalem were concerned that the will of their Lord was not to be trifled with. Thus, when the gospel was received by Samaritans as the result of the preaching of Philip, Peter and John were sent to confirm his work and to ensure the purity of the faith (Acts 8). When Peter extended the hand of fellowship to Cornelius and his household at Caesarea (Acts 10), it was a matter of concern to the Jerusalem church. Still later, when Paul and Barnabas preached in Asia Minor, and large numbers of Gentiles were received into the fellowship without the rite of circumcision, it was of such moment that a full-fledged convocation of the Church was held (Acts 15). Within the context of such a structured gathering, the Church sought the guidance of the Holy Spirit as it wrestled with the problem of radical commitment to the Christ. It concluded that no outward form should take precedence over primary commitment to Jesus Christ as Lord.

The appointment of missionaries—a familiar contemporary structural process—was begun in Antioch (Acts 13) in the midst of a prayer meeting. Somehow the Holy Spirit made it known to the congregation that in order to further their mission, and Christ's, they should set aside Paul and

Barnabas with their blessing—and no doubt their support (Acts 13). It seems significant that it was this missionary congregation which was so in tune with their Lord that they were derisively nicknamed "the Christ ones," Christians, and thereby gave the name to the whole movement.

The Pauline Church

In the New Testament period, as today, the missionary and benevolent enterprise necessitated considerable structure and promotion. Paul and Silas depended upon support from numerous congregations for their own work. They also solicited funds for the relief of the saints in Judea suffering from persecution and famine. Incidentally, some of their suffering may have resulted from their earlier communal experiment; but, if so, it did not deter Paul from laying their needs with enthusiasm upon the hearts of the churches. He did so even at the risk of jeopardizing his popularity with some of the brethren in his preaching.

Into a strategic situation like Corinth Paul did not leave to chance the development of the response he sought with regard to offering nor to the reception of his own services. He sent Titus and two anonymous brothers to prepare the way (II Corinthians 8). It is significant that Paul introduced these men as missionary associates "appointed by the churches" (note the plural) of Macedonia. They were to serve as messengers and in the work of finance so that there would be no blame attached in the administration of funds. Here, clearly, structure involved a number of congregations and was intended to extend the mission of the Church and to preserve the integrity of its work.

Structure for purposes of renewal and the deepening of the faith is also evident in the early Church. The return trips of Paul and Barnabas, and later of Paul and Silas, to their newly established congregations to train leaders and appoint overseers, were for this very purpose. Likewise, the admonition in the pastoral epistle of Titus to "appoint elders in every town" was an encouragement to extend structures for enrichment, renewal, purity of faith, and fulfillment of the basic mission.

From these brief samplings of a myriad of New Testament evidence one must conclude that structure is to the Church what the body is to the soul of a human being. Just as the body is part of the very essence of being human and provides opportunity both for sublimity and degradation in earthly life, so structure in the Church is part of the given circumstance of its existence and provides opportunity for the divine purposes to be fulfilled and the divine spirit to become incarnate or to be rejected. It is within this circumstance—not outside it—that effective criticism of the Church, and renewal of the faith, must take place.

Any denial of the validity of structure in the Church, "the body of Christ," is tantamount to a denial of the incarnation of Christ. Dean Ronald Osborn of Christian Theological Seminary reminds us that the Christian religion roots in creation, incarnation, and resurrection.[10] The Church has about it the earthiness of a stable and the smell of a dusty road, as well as the agony of a cross and the ineffable joy of an empty tomb. Its creative appropriation of the Holy Spirit was just as real in the hubbub and contention of apostles arguing with one another face to face in the structured conference at Jerusalem, as in any secluded prayer meeting ever held. Furthermore, the liberating effect of the corporate decision, corporately shared in the churches, has had a reverberating influence for good across the reaches of time and geography in the lives of men.

New Structures

The familiar term "body of Christ" implies structure and growth. It also connotes the redeeming ministry of Christ. The denomination which would clothe that concept with appropriate action can do so only as it gives attention to a structure which will make such action possible. The current interest in restructure in much of Protestantism is a wholesome recognition that in the dynamic changes of culture old structures become obsolete. When such obsolescence occurs, either there is a process of restructure, or the basic purpose for which the structures were originally created cannot be maintained.

Structure at the national or denominational level has many functions to fulfill. The more basic ones focus upon either the ministry of reconciliation in witness and service, or upon spiritual enrichment and the renewal of the Church. In either case, at their best they are designed to become a catalyst to stimulate throughout the whole of the church participation in and faithfulness to the Christian enterprise. When this happens, renewed congregations will tend to raise up discerning critics of the denominational structure and its leadership until it too experiences for itself some of the cleansing and renewing which must constantly be in process. When this does not happen the denomination tends to stagnate, atrophy, decline, and give evidence of the dry rot of lifeless form.

Denominational structures are Christ's instruments to the extent that they are responsive to the leading of his spirit and are responsible in their leadership. On the one hand they must make way for the Holy Spirit to become real in their objectives and sense of direction and, on the other hand, under his guidance they must employ the most responsible methodology which human ingenuity can devise. This is stewardship at its best. It is not an optional addition. Rather it is a fundamental characteristic of obedient responsiveness to the Lord of Life.

Integral to the function of denominational structure is that aspect of the work known as promotion. Its primary purpose (irrespective of any perversion) is the projection and articulation of the central mission of the Church. It is intended to stimulate corporate stewardship at the congregational level. Frequently it must prescribe for the myopia of congregational nearsightedness the bifocals of a faith which sees with sharpness and sensitivity the needs and opportunities of the immediate community and at the same time can look with clarity and understanding at the broad sweep of the gospel in global terms. The current promotional emphasis upon "fifty-fifty giving"—dividing the local budget with outreach—has been helpful at that point.

The word "promotion" is a combination of the two words "pro," meaning forward, and "motion," meaning movement. In the context of the interplay of denominational structure and congregational need for renewal and involvement, promotion becomes the clarion call to action. When both the denominational leadership and the promotional forces are consciously under the judgment of the Almighty, this call may well become the "Forward March!" of God. Truly, "The day of march has come."

Notes for Chapter 10

1. Colin W. Williams, *Where in the World?* (New York: National Council of Churches, 1963).
2. From p. 9 of *Beyond Religion* by Daniel Jenkins. Copyright © 1962 by Daniel Jenkins. The Westminster Press. Used by permission.
3. Jenkins, *op. cit.*, p. 11.
4. Dietrich Bonhoeffer, *Prisoner for God,* Letters and papers from prison, Eberhard Bethge, ed. (New York: The Macmillan Company, 1954), p. 167. By permission.

5. Bonhoeffer, *op. cit.*, p. 169.
6. *Church Dogmatics: Doctrine of Reconciliation* (New York: Charles Scribner's Sons, 1957).
7. Daniel Jenkins, *Beyond Religion* (Philadelphia: The Westminster Press, 1962), p. 16.
8. Nels Ferré, *The Sun and the Umbrella* (New York: Harper & Row, Publishers, Inc., 1953), p. 68. Used by permission.
9. Chapter 6 in *Religion and Culture: Essays in Honor of Paul Tillich,* Walter Leibrecht, ed. (New York: Harper & Row, Publishers, 1959).
10. Lecture on the nature of the Church, 1964, Louisville, Ky.

QUESTIONS FOR DISCUSSION

1. What is the basic difference between Catholics and Protestants on the doctrine of the church?
2. Is it possible to make an idol out of a congregation or a denomination?
3. What are some signs of health in Protestantism?
4. Are denominations necessary? What are the alternatives?
5. Does Christ's work require the large national and international church organizations that exist today?